ERNEST HEMINGWAY
AND THE PURSUIT OF HEROISM

Twentieth-Century American Writers

ERNEST HEMINGWAY
and the
PURSUIT OF HEROISM

By Leo Gurko

Thomas Y. Crowell Company, New York

Designed by Judie Mills
Manufactured in the United States of America
L. C. Card 68–21604
First Printing

Acknowledgments

Part of Chapter 6 appeared originally as an article in
the XVII (1955) issue of *College English,* and is
reprinted by permission of the National Council of
Teachers of English.

Quotations from the works of Ernest Hemingway are
protected by copyright and have been reprinted by
permission of Charles Scribner's Sons.

FOR MY MOTHER

TABLE OF CONTENTS

1 AN ADVENTUROUS LIFE

The forebears of talented men are not always talented themselves. The parents of Ernest Hemingway emphatically were. His father was a highly successful and unusually skillful doctor. A burly bearded man blessed with phenomenal eyesight, he had a great passion for hunting, fishing, and the outdoor life. He knew as much about guns and trout as about delivering babies, and was known equally for his achievements as a sportsman and obstetrician. Mrs. Hemingway was a singer, with a voice of operatic size. At the time of her marriage in 1896 she had a large number of voice pupils in Chicago and was earning a thousand dollars a month, a small fortune in those days.

They were also persons of very strong opinions, and by the time Ernest, their second child, was born on July 21, 1899, their ideas on how children should be brought up were firmly defined. They believed in the old-fashioned virtues: obedience, hard work, clean language, responsibility, ambition, decency, and morality. They wanted their children to be educated and make something of themselves. The youngsters were spanked when disobedient and encouraged to live as their parents and grandparents had lived before them. There was a great deal of energy in the bringing-up of the six young Hemingways but not much intellectual adventurousness.

There were also peculiarities. Mrs. Hemingway had wanted twins. When they did not materialize, she decided to bring up her first child, Marcelline, and her second, Ernest, as twins, though there was a year and a half between them. For a number of years they were dressed alike, treated alike, and given identical toys. Marcelline was kept in kindergarten for two years, until Ernest was old enough to enter the first grade with her. Thus the "twins" made their educational debut together. Dr. Hemingway also had a fixed idea that girls when they reached puberty were under a special emotional strain. He therefore kept his daughters out of school for a year when they reached the age of twelve or so and insisted that they remain quietly at home. What with such notions on the part of their parents, the four Hemingway girls had a hard time of it. There was a second Hemingway boy, Leicester, born fifteen years after Ernest, a gap that all but made them members of different generations. While growing up, Ernest was in effect practically an only son.

Like most parents, the Hemingways imposed, or tried to impose, their convictions and accomplishments upon their offspring. The mother, faithful to her musical interests, recruited a chamber-music group from the ranks of her family. Marcelline was taught the violin and viola; Ernest, the cello. They often played quartets, with Mrs. Hemingway at the piano and the father at the cornet. Ernest disliked the cello intensely. He had no aptitude for it, and cared little for music altogether. His mother's large music room, with its raised platform for recitals, was for him a torture chamber until he abandoned music and began using the room for boxing practice. Mrs. Hemingway was also devoutly religious. She sang in the choir of the Congregational church and brought up all six of her children as believers. But with Ernest at any rate, religion—at least as his mother conceived it—took no more hold than music.

In one respect his father's influence was more successful. Dr. Hemingway was a nature lover. He knew the names of all the birds and flowers, and was enthusiastic about everything he saw. Nature as a source of refreshment for the senses and spirit, as indeed a kind of Garden of Eden to which men returned for healing, took profound hold of Ernest. His father's response to nature was also intensely active. One did not just sit and contemplate it but thrashed around in it as vigorously as possible. Walking, hunting, camping, fishing were Dr. Hemingway's familiar points of entry into the countryside. They were to be his elder son's as well. For Ernest they were indeed to become arts deserving the closest attention, study, and care, to be practised as skillfully as possible not only for the immediate pleasure, but for the pure joy of doing something well, and because in some deeper sense they released the soul.

In other areas Dr. Hemingway's influence was less fruitful. He himself had been taught to believe that dancing, card-playing, gambling, and drinking hard liquor were sinful. Sex as a subject was strictly forbidden, and though he delivered three thousand babies during his career, discussion of the biological processes was wholly taboo. Hemingway did not accept these views, and in his story "Fathers and Sons" he expresses through his young hero Nick Adams his confusion and revolt against such paternal dicta. In another of the Nick Adams stories, "The Doctor and the Doctor's Wife," he casts doubt on his father's physical courage —a surprising attitude in view of Dr. Hemingway's masculine vigor and impressive physical prowess.

Though Hemingway's parents shared the same views, they did not really have the same interests, and it is remarkable that two such highly developed personalities should have lived together for more than thirty years and raised six children with so little quarreling, so few overt clashes, and so little disturbance of the surface of their married life. But the tensions below the visible surface were powerful. Mrs. Hemingway felt that marriage had deprived her of a career as a concert singer. Dr. Hemingway had wanted to practise a more adventurous medicine than was possible in a comfortable, middle-class town. His brother had become a medical missionary. He himself had longed to be a doctor in Guam or Greenland, or failing these remote places, at least in some rough frontier area like Nevada. He had to give up this dream upon marriage. His wife needed culture and civilization. There would be precious little music in Nevada and no Christianity at all in Guam. Instead they began their married life in Chicago, each with a not wholly suppressed feeling of self-sacrifice.

They soon moved from Chicago to a house in Oak Park, a well-to-do suburb west of the city. Oak Park carefully distinguished itself from Chicago as a community "where the saloons end and the churches begin." It was a model of high-minded propriety. The streets were clean, the houses and lawns well tended, the incidence of crime and juvenile delinquency low, the average income high, the sense of civic pride tremendous. The Hemingways could not have picked a more characteristically and ideally American place to settle in. Against this background of conventional respectability, Ernest grew up in a conventionally respectable way. He went to grammar school and attended church. Summers were spent on Walloon Lake, in a section of northern Michigan still inhabited by the Ojibway Indians, where Dr. Hemingway, with his love for the outdoors, had bought a house.

In high school Ernest played football, was a reporter on the school paper, and wrote little satirical pieces for the school magazine in the style of Ring Lardner, the sports reporter just then bringing out his acid little stories about big-time athletes. He did not, however, excel at team sports, but soon developed an interest in boxing, where everything depended solely on his own skill. The sport that pitted one antagonist against another—the two boxers in the ring, the man and the animal in hunting, the man and the fish in fishing, the matador and the bull in bullfighting—fascinated young Hemingway, and it was these personal, one-to-one confrontations that were to provide his art with its central drama.

He injured an eye in football and damaged it again while boxing—the first of many injuries he was to endure throughout his life. He was indeed mysteriously accident-prone, as though secretly wanting to expose himself to danger, thereby testing his ability to absorb punishment.

Despite his participation in school activities, he had the temperament of a loner. He knew everyone in Oak

Park but made few friends and none that survived into later life. And there grew in him the conviction that there was more to the world than Oak Park, that his father's beliefs and his mother's prescriptions were not the all-in-all of experience, that in fact the society into which he had been born was a narrow one and could not hold him forever. On two occasions he ran away from home and went on the road, hopping freights, washing dishes in cheap cafés, working on the docks, and even boxing for a living.

In June 1917, just before turning eighteen, he was graduated from Oak Park High School. He had made little impression upon the school. One of his English teachers remembered him as having a certain flair for writing. Except for that and the fact that he was taller and huskier than most of his classmates, he seems to have been indistinguishably average.

There now came the first serious break between his parents' conception of his life and his own. They wanted him to go to college; he refused. He insisted instead on enlisting in the American army; the country had actively entered the First World War the previous April. But the damaged eye barred him from service. This rebuff was a sharp disappointment. It was not only that, like his father, he craved action and adventure, but that service in France was then regarded by a whole generation of American youth as a romantic call to arms. The men sent overseas were envied while those left behind—like Hemingway, F. Scott Fitzgerald, and Thomas Wolfe among those who were later to become writers—felt painfully let down. Such feelings about war were the last of their kind to be held by Americans, just as the First World War was the last about which it was possible to be romantic.

Ernest's rejection by the army did not make him more receptive to the idea of college. Despite family opposition he was resolved to go off on his own. Mrs. Hemingway had a brother in Kansas City, and in the late summer of 1917 Ernest went to stay with him while looking for a job. He found one as a cub reporter on the Kansas City *Star,* at that time one of the great newspapers in the country. The *Star* prided itself not alone on the accuracy of its news coverage but on the pithy simplicity of its prose. A list of rules issued to all new editorial employees included the strictures: Be brief; be simple; be clear. Brevity, simplicity, and clarity were to be among the supreme virtues of Hemingway's own writing. They were drummed into him not as lessons in a schoolroom, but as professional instructions that he had to obey if he were to hold his job.

He began by covering fires, then was assigned to

the police and hospital beat. Here, at eighteen, he was exposed—perhaps too soon—to life and death at their most savage. He had had a taste of illness and pain while accompanying his father on medical calls to the Ojibways during the summers of his boyhood—an experience savagely recalled in his story "Indian Camp." But in Kansas City he witnessed the full range of human misery, from the distorted lives of criminals to the shattered bodies of hospital inmates.

He was also exposed to the habits and attitudes of newspaper reporters. These men, to protect themselves from the horrors in which they were daily immersed, developed an outer shell of cynicism and toughness, though inwardly they were often tender and senti-mental. Many of them were also novelists or would-be novelists or disappointed novelists. Since the days of Mark Twain and Stephen Crane, newspapers had sup-plied both training and occupation for American writers, a role now taken over by the universities. Hemingway began with a newspaper that made a special cult of style; he himself was to develop into a great stylist. His first professional comrades were men to whom the act of creative writing, as distinguished from journalism, was a perfectly natural one. He also adopted, at an impressionable age, the combination of toughness and tenderness that marked their reaction to the wounded world. Later, a famous *New Yorker* cartoon was to depict a hairy muscular forearm with a huge hand holding a rose. The caption underneath read: "The Soul of Ernest Hemingway."

Through all his months on the *Star* the urge to get into the European war remained alive in Ernest. He discovered other means of joining aside from army enlistment. One route was through the American Red Cross, which needed ambulance drivers and medical aides. In the spring of 1918 Ernest left the *Star* and signed on with the Red Cross. He returned home briefly to say good-bye to his family, then departed for New York and the boat to Europe. On arriving overseas, he was sent to the Italian front. In June, a month short of his nineteenth birthday, he found himself immediately behind the lines, distributing Red Cross packages to Italian soldiers in the trenches. The Austrian army was dug in a few hundred yards away.

So far the whole experience had been more of a lark than anything else. But on July 6, in the tiny village of Fossalta di Piave, it suddenly changed. Hemingway was handing out chocolate bars to a group of Italian soldiers when an Austrian mortar shell exploded squarely in the trench where he was standing. The Italian soldier on one side of him was killed outright. The soldier on the other side fell to the ground, both legs badly shattered. Dozens of shell fragments penetrated Hemingway's left leg; he fainted from shock. When he came to, it seemed to him that his soul, like a handkerchief blown away by a sudden gust of wind, had left his body and that at the last moment he had reached out and pulled it back. Like Lieutenant Henry, the American in *A Farewell to Arms* who was similarly wounded, he reached down to feel his knee but could not find it. He heard the wounded soldier groaning next to him. In a daze, scarcely conscious of his movements, he somehow got to his feet, heaved the wounded man over his shoulders, and began stumbling back toward the rear. On the way he fainted again, recovered, and went on. He finally reached a first-aid station back of the front lines, and there deposited his burden. The man was dead, and Hemingway, what with shock, exhaustion, and loss of blood, nearly so.

He was removed to a field hospital, and his wounds attended to. Numerous pieces of shrapnel were taken out of his injured leg. Some, however, too deeply embedded, had to be left in, and these steel fragments were to trouble Hemingway for the rest of his life. When he was well enough to be moved again, he was taken to a military hospital in Milan. He spent several weeks convalescing there, and then received a double reward. The Italian government gave him a medal for valor in the field and allowed him, though a foreigner, to enlist as an infantryman in the Italian army. Thus he became a soldier and a military hero simultaneously—and both at nineteen.

One of the volunteer nurses attending Hemingway at the hospital in Milan was an American girl with the exotic name of Agnes H. von Kurowsky. She was some years older than Ernest. At first she was his nurse, then his friend; then he fell in love with her. Her feelings for him, while warm, were less intense. But their presence in Italy, in their extreme youth and under the excitation of the war, lent their romance an extraordinary bloom. The passionate responsiveness, violence, and sensuality of Italy made a profound impact on Hemingway and shook him loose from whatever linkages remained with the world of Oak Park. Before leaving for the front again, this time as a combat soldier, he proposed to Agnes. She turned him down.

The war ended soon afterward. Before leaving Italy, he proposed to Agnes again, was again refused. When he got back to Oak Park in 1919, he proposed again by letter and was once more refused. He then had to get used to the idea that Agnes was beyond reach. It was painful, but Ernest slowly got over her. Everything that had happened to him from the moment he reached Italy—the war, the wound, the love affair, the Italians, the military life—would within ten years be poured into his famous novel about the First World War, *A Farewell to Arms*.

When Hemingway returned home after the war, he was greeted as a hero. Parties were given for him. He was invited to address the graduating class at his high school. His medals were much admired. But these festivities soon came to an end, and the fuss over him died down. Oak Park settled back to its normal routines, and Ernest was left to himself with nothing that he wanted to do. Like thousands of soldiers all over the country, he was at loose ends, finding it difficult to get back to civilian life after the end of the war. Hemingway's particularly bad case of postwar jitters was described with special delicacy and insight in his story "Soldier's Home."

How to occupy his days became an almost insoluble problem. He went out and boxed occasionally, but most of the time he just hung around the house. His four-year-old brother Leicester idolized him, but the adulation of a small boy was hardly enough to sustain him. His parents wanted him to get a job, but the idea of doing routine work in Oak Park was repulsive to him. His parents again urged him to go to college and train for a profession. Ernest again refused. He would accept his father's advice and example on hunting and fishing, but on little else. In Italy the sense of life as both an adventure and a tragedy had grown upon him. In Oak Park it was neither. It was this conviction more than anything else that unfitted him for an ordinary existence at home.

There now ensued a difficult and wretched time. The older Hemingways regarded their son's idleness with mounting unhappiness. Dr. Hemingway could not understand how a young man of twenty, especially his own son, could just sit about doing nothing. Ernest was obviously out of joint with everything. His experience abroad had spoiled him for Oak Park and Oak Park for him. He wanted to do something meaningful and exciting with his life, but what exactly he had no idea. So he stayed at home, killing time, and making himself and everyone else miserable.

This stalemate continued through the summer of 1919. When the season at Walloon Lake was over and the other Hemingways returned to Oak Park, Ernest stayed on in northern Michigan. He rented a room in a boarding house in Petoskey—the locale of his first novel *The Torrents of Spring*—and began writing poems and short stories. This, at least, gave him an excuse to get away from his family. His parents regarded his writing as pointless, as another sign of the waste and futility of his existence. When his pieces were rejected by the magazine editors to whom he sent them, Ernest was almost inclined to agree.

Early in 1920 he left Petoskey and went to Toronto in search of a job. He had had one satisfying experience on a newspaper, and now he found another as a reporter for the Toronto *Star Weekly*. Style was emphasized less than on the Kansas City *Star,* but Ernest was not tied down to the grim facts of a hospital beat. Instead he was encouraged to dig up events and write features of general interest, and was given a chance to express his sense of humor and irony. For the first time articles began appearing under his own by-line, Ernest M. Hemingway, the *M* standing for Miller, a letter that vanished when his books came out.

The news of his employment, when it reached home, cheered his parents up a bit, but in the late spring of 1920 Ernest gave up his reporting and returned to Oak Park. That summer Dr. Hemingway was unable to make the annual pilgrimage to Walloon Lake, and Ernest promised that he would do the chores and be responsible for the place in his father's absence. The summer was disastrous. Ernest did none of the necessary work and disappeared for days at a stretch with a couple of cronies. They would appear for meals and leave immediately afterward. Mrs. Hemingway grew more and more irritated. The house was too much for her to manage alone. After a final bitter quarrel with Ernest over his irresponsibility, she wrote him a letter literally throwing him out of the house and forbidding him to return unless his attitude changed. The letter was dated July 21, 1920—Ernest's twenty-first birthday. In his family's eyes he seemed well on his way to becoming a drifter or bum, or in the expression in common use then, a ne'er-do-well.

The quarrel had a chastening effect on Ernest, for in the fall of 1920 he did at last get a job in Chicago, writing advertising copy for a real-estate firm. He found the work uninspiring, but it left him plenty of free time and energy for other things. He began to write again, producing sketches, anecdotes, and short stories, chiefly about the events he remembered from his summers among the Ojibways and his year in Europe during the war.

Chicago was then coming to the end of its literary renaissance. It had passed through a period of phenomenal growth to become the nation's second city; its physical expansion had been accompanied by an equally striking expansion in architecture, opera, literature, and the general ferment of ideas. It had become a magnet for talented and artistically inclined young men from all over the Midwest—Sherwood Anderson, Frank Lloyd Wright, Theodore Dreiser, Edgar Lee Masters, Floyd Dell, Sinclair Lewis, Ben Hecht, Carl Sandburg, among others.

Hemingway gravitated into the literary circle almost at once. The man with whom he became most intimate was Sherwood Anderson, whose collection of tales about life in a small town, *Winesburg, Ohio,* had appeared the year before and made him famous. He was a warmhearted, generous, genial man with an unaffected interest in other writers and particularly in younger ones, whom he was anxious to encourage. Literature was more than a profession to him. It was an escape from his dreary life as a businessman in Ohio.

He had brought a fresh note to American fiction: the direct statement of immediate emotion in sentences that were brief, stripped, and economical. The long, complex, zigzag sentences of the classic American novelists—Hawthorne, Melville, and particularly Henry James—were suitable instruments for communicating ideas and observations. Anderson believed that thinking got in the way of feeling and sense impression, which to him were the decisive elements in human life. He wanted to free them from interference of any kind. He wrote as his characters felt, in quick exhalations, in brief, even monotonous spurts of prose that, on first appearance, seemed more natural and lifelike than the formal literary manner of the earlier age. Anderson himself had learned something from Gertrude Stein whose fictional sketches, *Three Lives* (1909), tried to capture the movements of the mind in fixed rhythmic word patterns. Another of his models was

James Joyce's *Portrait of the Artist As a Young Man* (1914), with its frequent stream-of-consciousness passages registering the waves of reverie as they floated or rushed through the hero's mind.

Having learned from his predecessors, Anderson was eager to pass on the secrets of the new impressionism to his followers. In Hemingway he found a willing and enthusiastic pupil. The life of sensation as distinct from thought had already impressed itself on Hemingway as being the more real. What he felt in his flesh was far more vivid and intense than his reflections about it. Without thinking of it in these terms, he reversed Plato's doctrine. To Plato the senses were treacherous and the mind nobly permanent. To Hemingway the mind was treacherous and abstract, the senses, in their concreteness and immediacy, were always to be trusted, and he resolved to place them at the center of his writing. Since Sherwood Anderson was doing so already in his own way, Hemingway attached himself to the older man as a natural guide.

Anderson had returned from Europe not long before and urged upon Hemingway the advantages of living in Paris. Hemingway needed no urging. His first stay in Europe had intoxicated him with Italy, and he was quite prepared to embrace France. Paris was the city for young writers and artists. It was intellectually alive. It was also particularly inexpensive for Americans. Anderson promised him letters of introduction, especially to Gertrude Stein who had settled in France before the war and knew everyone.

Hemingway also met in Chicago a young pianist from St. Louis named Hadley Richardson and promptly fell in love with her. He proposed to her, as he had earlier to Agnes von Kurowsky, and this time he was accepted. It was now the spring of 1921, one of the happiest times in Hemingway's life. He was young. He had emerged from the depression that had seized him after the war. He had begun to write and was being encouraged by successful writers older than himself. He was in love and his love was returned.

Full of buoyant vitality, he began to consider quitting his advertising job and going back to newspaper work. He had enjoyed his experiences as a reporter, and felt that of all occupations reporting was probably closest to creative writing.

In September 1921 he and Hadley were married. With the older Hemingways present, the ceremony took place in the Methodist church at Horton Bay, a village near Walloon Lake. Hemingway and his parents had been reconciled almost from the time that he began working in Chicago. They thoroughly approved of Hadley and of marriage. After a brief honeymoon in the Hemingways' summer home, the young couple set off for Toronto where Ernest, having quit his job in Chicago, resumed his earlier connection with the *Star Weekly*. He enjoyed his new work, but his real ambition was to get to Europe as soon as possible. In December 1921 he was offered a post as foreign correspondent by a sister newspaper, the *Daily Star,* which he accepted eagerly. That same month he and Hadley, armed with letters of introduction given them by Anderson, set sail for France.

Hemingway was twenty-two, as tall as his father though not yet as burly. He was lithe, quick, and graceful in his movements, with the look of a "sleepy panther," in the phrase of Archibald MacLeish. He and Hadley were about to enter Paris at the start of its most glittering and active period for expatriate Americans.

Paris in the 1920s was everyone's catalyst. It was the experimental and fermenting center of every art. It was highly sophisticated, yet broke up naturally into small intimate *quartiers.* Its cafés were hotbeds of intellectual and social energy, pent up during the war and now released. Young people from all over the world flocked to Paris, drawn not only by the city's intrinsic attractions but by the devaluation of the franc.

The young Hemingways settled on the Left Bank, and since they were short of money, rented modest rooms in an ancient walk-up. They moved several times, taking flats that were usually on the top floor, five or six flights up, commanding good views of the roofs of Paris. This was somehow in tune with a passion to absorb the city. Hemingway did much of his writing in cafés, where he would sit for hours over a beer or *Pernod* with paper spread before him. He took long walks through the streets and gardens, lingered over the Cézannes in the Luxembourg Museum, and let the great city permeate his senses.

He met Gertrude Stein through Anderson's introduction, and a friendship began that was to continue for the next three or four years. Miss Stein and her companion, Alice B. Toklas, exchanged visits with the Hemingways. Ernest and Gertrude talked endlessly about writing, or rather she did most of the talking while he listened. Her apartment at 27 rue de Fleurus was filled with magnificent canvases by the modern painters, including the famous portrait of her by Picasso. It was also filled with Miss Stein's unpublished manuscripts. One of these, *The Making of Americans,* Hemingway would eventually take in hand and see through to its publication in Ford Madox Ford's magazine *transatlantic review.*

Meanwhile, in 1922 and 1923, he roamed through Europe on free-lance assignments for the Toronto *Daily Star.* He covered various political conferences in Germany, Italy, and the Near East. He interviewed

Mussolini, Clemenceau, and Lloyd George. He was in Germany during the catastrophic inflation of 1923. He went to Spain and discovered bullfighting. All over the continent he witnessed the crazy-quilt frontier arrangements of the Versailles Treaty, already laying the groundwork for the next war. And in 1922 he covered the bloody conflict between Turkey and Greece, in which thousands of Greek refugees were expelled from Turkey to make their painful tragic way across Thrace. Incidents from this war provided Hemingway with many of the transitional sketches in his short-story collection *In Our Time.*

When the weather turned cold in the late fall, Hadley and Ernest, both of whom loved skiing, began taking trips to the Swiss and Austrian mountains. One day in 1922 Hadley left Paris to join Ernest in Switzerland. While she waited for the train in the Gare de Lyon, her valise containing the manuscripts of virtually all of Hemingway's stories disappeared. Whether stolen or mislaid, it was never recovered. One of the cruelest moments in their lives came when she broke the news to him. After the first shock he went painfully to work rewriting as many of the stories as memory and imagination made possible.

In Paris he made friends with the poet Ezra Pound, with whom he often boxed and played tennis, and occasionally discussed literature. He also met James

Joyce and came to admire him tremendously as a writer. They never discussed literature, mainly because Joyce seldom discussed literature with anyone. Hemingway, devoted as ever to sports, went to the fights and attended the races. He had a passion for betting on the horses, and working out betting systems was one of his favorite ways of relaxing from the strain of writing.

He was becoming increasingly devoted to imaginative writing, to the point where his newspaper assignments and the need to grind out journalistic pieces were growing more and more irksome. Another threat to his work was the "arty" atmosphere of Paris. The cafés of the city, he soon recognized, were filled with aesthetes of one kind or another who wanted to be artists, talked incessantly and even knowledgeably about art, but never really produced anything. There were a hundred of these clever loafers and dilettantes for every real writer. Hemingway developed a contempt and even fear of them, perhaps because there was in him, as in most genuine artists, a feeling of uncertainty about his own talent. He drove himself to hard work and avoided the café crowd as much as he could.

His work was now being accepted for the first time and began to appear in the little magazines. Six of his poems were printed in the January 1923 issue of Harriet Monroe's magazine *Poetry*. In the summer of 1923 a friend of his, Robert McAlmon, brought out a 300-copy edition of Hemingway's first book, a small volume called *Three Stories and Ten Poems*. In January 1924 another friend, William Bird, owner of the Three Mountains Press in Paris, published a second small book, *In Our Time,* containing sketches drawn from Hemingway's experiences in the First War, in the more recent Greco-Turkish war, and with Spanish bullfighting. This volume came to all of thirty-two pages, in an edition of 170 copies.

The sense of creative achievement was rapidly bringing Hemingway to a crisis about his newspaper work. Gertrude Stein had warned him that journalism and imaginative writing did not mix, and that one would be sure to drive out the other. He did not need much persuading. Some years later he remarked in *Death in the Afternoon:* "In writing for a newspaper you told what happened and, with one trick and another, you communicated the emotion aided by the element of timeliness which gives a certain emotion to any account of something that has happened on that day; but the real thing, the sequence of motion and fact which made the emotion and which would be as valid in a year or in ten years or, with luck and if you stated it purely enough, always, was beyond me and I was working very hard to try to get it." It was this "real thing" he was now ready to concentrate on exclusively.

In the middle of 1923 he informed Miss Stein bitterly that Hadley was pregnant, and that he was not ready to be a father. She urged him to go back to Toronto, work hard and save up money, then quit journalism, return to Europe, and risk it as a writer. He agreed. In the fall of 1923 the Hemingways were back in Toronto, where Ernest once again accepted a steady job with the *Star*. They saved as much as they could, and awaited the birth of their baby. It was a boy, christened John, whom they promptly nicknamed Bumby, and early in 1924, with Bumby in hand, they were back in Paris.

They settled down above a sawmill at 113 rue Notre Dame des Champs, a small winding street halfway between the Boulevard St. Michel and the Boulevard Raspail. It was to the whirring of the sawmill and the pervasive smell of freshly cut wood that Hemingway resumed his now single-minded pursuit of writing. Gertrude Stein and Alice Toklas formally became godparents to Bumby. They noted with approval the appearance of a family cat, archly referred to as F. Puss, and Hemingway's amiable acceptance of fatherhood.

The one big problem was to make the money hold

out. The Hemingways put themselves on short rations, ate, drank, and entertained as little as possible, pounced eagerly on the small checks that arrived in the mail as payment for accepted stories, and were intensely conscious of being poor. The sensation was not altogether unpleasant. Their extreme youth, the excitement of living abroad, the sense of making a fresh start, even the unexpected joy of parenthood, gave their poverty a romantic flavor.

Nearly all of Hemingway's published writing had appeared first in Europe. In America he was still largely ignored by publishers and readers. But he was beginning to be known by a few alert critics and fellow writers, who spread word back home about the appearance of an arresting new personality. Sherwood Anderson was immensely pleased by the success of his protégé, and urged his New York publishers, Boni and Liveright, to bring out a volume of Hemingway's stories. At last, in October 1925, they yielded to his persuasion and printed the first American edition of *In Our Time*. It was the first of Hemingway's books to appear in his own country. The volume contained all the sketches of the Bird edition, two of the three stories in the earlier book printed by McAlmon, and ten new stories—most of them having Nick Adams as the central figure.

Another of Hemingway's American sponsors was

F. Scott Fitzgerald. Like Anderson he was extremely generous in his responses to other writers. He had admired Hemingway's work long before meeting its author, and urged Maxwell Perkins, his editor at Scribner's, to bid for it. When Fitzgerald went to Paris in the spring of 1925, he looked up Hemingway at once and suggested to him the advantages of switching publishers. Hemingway was moved by Fitzgerald's enthusiasm and admiration. It was obvious that the older writer's feelings were disinterested. Fitzgerald had nothing personally to gain from boosting Hemingway, and was himself already famous since the publication in 1920 of his first novel, *This Side of Paradise*. He was soon to become more so with the appearance of his third novel, *The Great Gatsby*. He and Hemingway became warm friends.

There grew in Hemingway through 1924 and the early months of 1925 the desire to try his hand at something longer, more ambitious, and more complex than the short story, to launch into a first novel. Every July for some years he had gone to Spain, attending the festival of San Fermin in Pamplona, with its seven days of bullfighting, revelry, and religious celebration. This festival became the climactic event of the novel he began writing in the summer of 1925, which he called *The Sun Also Rises*. He wrote the first draft in a swift five weeks, then spent five long agonizing months in extensive revisions. As a break from this labor, he interrupted the revising process in November 1925 to dash off—this time in a single week—a short, blistering little parody, part novel, part sketch, part spoof, named *The Torrents of Spring*. This short piece was both a climax and a turning point in Hemingway's relationship with his literary friends.

By the end of 1925 his friendship with Gertrude Stein had reached a critical stage. It had always contained an irritating element for him. He felt Miss Stein wanted disciples, not friends. He found her highly intelligent but also highly egotistical and patronizing, inclined to praise only those writers to whom she could feel superior or whose standing had fallen off. He was also pained by her assumption that he had learned writing from her, that without her tutelage he would not have amounted to anything. Hemingway himself was hypersensitive and thin-skinned, with a fierce sense of his own identity and worth. He was quick to take offense at any challenge to himself, whether to his person (when he would retaliate with his fists) or to his talent (when he would retaliate with his pen). It was hence inevitable that sooner or later he and Miss Stein would quarrel. As he grew more independent of her, as his own literary reputation began to spread, the latent hostility between them came to the surface. The final break was precipitated by Miss Stein's remark that underneath his surface bravado and cult of manliness, Hemingway was really "yellow." No other charge, not even that of mediocrity as a writer, could have wounded him more painfully.

His friendship with Sherwood Anderson came to an end at about the same time, and here Hemingway was the aggressor. People kept labeling Hemingway as Anderson's disciple, and the thought of being anyone's disciple was more than the younger man, once he began to sense his own powers, could tolerate. He wanted to be his own man, not only in his own eyes but in the eyes of the world. So he repudiated Anderson publicly, not by any direct statement but in a manner far more devastating. He wrote *The Torrents of Spring,* which ridiculed and parodied Anderson's style of writing, his characters, and his most cherished ideas about life. After the book appeared in the spring of 1926, the tie between Anderson and Hemingway was definitely broken. Later, Hemingway somewhat lamely sought to justify his attack by saying that after *Winesburg, Ohio* Anderson had lapsed into pulpy sentiment, that in later novels like *Dark Laughter* and *Many Marriages* he was unconsciously caricaturing himself. Such remarks only aggravated Anderson further.

Yet it was this painful affair that made it possible

for Hemingway to change publishers and to carry out Fitzgerald's fervent hope that he join him at Scribner's. Boni and Liveright had published *In Our Time* and taken out options on Hemingway's next two books only at Anderson's urging. When they got wind of *The Torrents of Spring,* they naturally refused to have anything to do with such an attack upon their chief literary property. Scribner's was not enthusiastic about publishing the book either, but in order to acquire the rights to *The Sun Also Rises* they reluctantly agreed to print *The Torrents of Spring.* Neither *In Our Time* nor *The Torrents of Spring* sold well, nor for that matter did *The Sun Also Rises* when it first came out in October 1926. But all of them were steadily preparing the ground for Hemingway's popular success, a success that would come by the end of the decade.

The relationship with Fitzgerald, too, was not without its difficulties. Hemingway took an almost instant dislike to his friend's beautiful and talented wife, the unhappy Zelda Fitzgerald. He thought that she was jealous of Fitzgerald's talent and success as a writer, that she was driving him to write trashy stories for the popular magazines to pay for her extravagant standard of living, that she was probably mad and would be sure to ruin him. In a few years Zelda would indeed go mad, yet Hemingway's conviction was less a stroke of profound psychological insight than an expression of his personal dislike. Fitzgerald was deeply attached to his wife, and was made unhappy by the friction that arose when they and the Hemingways were together. This did not, however, prevent him from seeing as much of Hemingway as he could, alone when possible, and cultivating a relationship between them that produced a brilliant exchange of letters over the years.

In the meantime, during this period of difficult personal situations, Hemingway was falling out of love with Hadley. He had met another young woman, Pauline Pfeiffer, a fashion designer from St. Louis (curiously, Hemingway's first three wives were all young women from St. Louis), and proceeded to fall in love with her. In 1927 he and Hadley were divorced, and he married Pauline. His second wife was a Roman Catholic, and Hemingway became converted to Catholicism after marrying her. Under the circumstances the parting with Hadley was relatively amicable, and Hemingway was free to see Bumby as often as he wished.

During the interval between marriages Hemingway lived alone in Paris and continued to write short stories. Late in 1927 a second collection of these was published by Scribner's under the title *Men Without Women*. It included, among other famous stories, "The Killers," "Fifty Grand," "In Another Country," and "The Undefeated." The subjects of these four—

gangsters, prizefighters, soldiers, and bullfighters—
were handled superbly, and were strikingly characteristic of Hemingway's choice of material. His literary
reputation was already established by the time this
volume appeared, and though this was not immediately
reflected in sales, there had been a steady progression
in the size of the first printings of his books. The
American edition of *In Our Time* was less than fifteen
hundred copies. *The Sun Also Rises* exceeded five
thousand. *Men Without Women* came to more than
seven thousand. None of these amounted to very much
in terms of royalties, though together with magazine
sales they were enough to earn Hemingway a modest
living. But they were an index to his expanding position as a professional writer and a key to his forth-
coming breakthrough to the status of a best-selling
author.

By the end of 1927 Ernest and Pauline were married, and Hemingway's life as an American expatriate
in Paris was virtually over. It was not so much that
Paris had lost its charm for him—he returned to it
a number of times afterward—as that it seemed appropriate to begin his new marriage with a change of
scene. They returned to the United States and settled
down in Key West, Florida, which was to be their
home for the next ten years. Key West was on the Gulf

of Mexico where Ernest could go deep-sea fishing, a sport that he found both relaxing and dramatic. The area had a large Spanish-speaking population and was close to Cuba and the other Spanish-speaking islands in the Caribbean. Hemingway, who by this time spoke Spanish fluently and had developed a profound affection for Spain and the Spaniards, found all this congenial.

The house he bought in Key West was a nine-room limestone that commanded a spectacular view of the Gulf; to it he added an enormous swimming pool with underwater lights. In Europe he had developed a taste for fountains and now had two of his own constructed, one a replica of the pre-Civil War vessel *Mississippi,* the other made from a large Spanish olive jar and Spanish tiles. The house itself was filled with Spanish furniture, tiles, and woven mats, Venetian glass chandeliers, and mounted specimens of animals and fish.

Hemingway would write in the morning and go fishing in the afternoon. The sea absorbed him almost as much as his writing desk. "It's the last free place, the sea," he once observed. He had begun work on a new novel, *A Farewell to Arms,* and spent almost the whole of 1928 writing it. In that year Pauline gave birth to Hemingway's second son, Patrick, a blissful event that was almost overshadowed by a shattering tragedy near the end of the year, a tragedy which would affect

Hemingway to the end of his life. On December 6 his father committed suicide.

Dr. Hemingway had been under growing nervous strain during the twenties. His health, superb to begin with and in which he took an almost naïve joy, began to fail. He developed heart trouble, and like so many men inordinately proud of their physical well-being, refused to take care of the condition and even at times refused to acknowledge it. He had also invested heavily in the Florida real-estate boom, hoping to make enough money to retire on, and when the boom collapsed, he was very hard hit. He fell into depression and acute melancholia, from which nothing could rouse him. One morning he went up to his study and shot himself, using one of the several guns about the house, the guns he had handled so expertly and in whose use he had so expertly trained Ernest.

The impact of the suicide on Ernest was incalculable. He grieved over his father's death, but he was also profoundly disturbed by the question of his father's courage, or lack of it. Courage, the ability to absorb punishment unflinchingly, or as Hemingway defined it on one occasion, grace under pressure, was a virtue that he greatly admired and that his father had taught him to admire. Yet under extreme pressure his father had buckled and collapsed. He could not help feeling that his father had failed in an essential aspect of living. That he had not only failed but had somehow failed him, Ernest, and that this failure was in a direct sense a challenge to himself. The flaw in the father alerted the son more keenly than ever to a concern over his own moral and emotional strength. It was soon afterward that Ernest assumed the nickname of Papa, by which he was familiarly known to the end of his life, almost as though he were assuming the burden of being the ideal papa that his own father had failed to be. And ten years later in his novel about Spain, *For Whom the Bell Tolls,* Robert Jordan, the protagonist, broods recurrently over his father's suicide and at a crucial point debates whether he should follow the same course.

Ernest went to Oak Park for the funeral. Soon afterward, he and Pauline set up a large trust fund for the support of his widowed mother. Pauline, who had independent means and was very fond of Mrs. Hemingway, contributed a large share. Reminiscing with his family about the past, Ernest learned how his father had reacted to the receipt of his books. McAlmon had sent him a half-dozen copies of *Three Stories and Ten Poems.* Dr. Hemingway had been so offended by their harsh and occasionally profane language that, in indignation, he wrapped the books up again and sent them back to Paris. He also disapproved of what he regarded as the neurotic behavior and sexually de-

praved actions of the characters in *The Sun Also Rises.*
Yet he was secretly proud of Ernest's success, and
would sneak into Chicago bookstores to gaze gratify-
ingly at the display of his son's books. This ambivalent
reaction on the father's part was in its small way an
exact reflection of the whole relationship between
them, which was a subtle amalgam of pride, affection,
and mistrust.

In the spring of 1929, Ernest was back in Paris,
correcting proofs on the new novel. He lingered on
for part of the summer, revisiting Spain, trotting about
with the Fitzgeralds, and boxing with Morley Callaghan, a young Canadian writer whom he knew from the
early days in Toronto. In his memoir on Hemingway,
Callaghan testified to his friend's touchiness and mood-
iness, his baffling shifts between friendliness and hostility. It was an especially difficult period in Hemingway's life, but his spirits picked up with the publication of *A Farewell to Arms* late in September 1929.
The book appeared a few days before the historic
stock-market crash that formally ushered in the great
depression. Yet the novel itself was a great popular
success. More than thirty thousand copies were printed
to begin with, and by February of the following year
eighty thousand copies had been sold.

Hemingway liked to think of *A Farewell to Arms*
as his version of *Romeo and Juliet.* The scene of both

is Italy. Lieutenant Henry and Catherine Barkley are certainly "star-crossed lovers." The First World War is the modern equivalent of the feud between the Montagues and Capulets, and Hemingway's lovers retreat from it and sign their separate peace as do Shakespeare's. Even Shakespeare's supporting characters—Mercutio, Friar Laurence, and Juliet's nurse—have their obvious equivalents in the novel. The tone of the two is much the same, the peculiar pathos of young love flowering in a hostile universe. The novel is filled with remarkable descriptions of war on the Italian front, superbly fused with the private lives of hero and heroine. The aesthetic success of the novel brought Hemingway to the height of his fame and power as a writer, while its financial success freed him from the poverty and enforced economies of his expatriate years. He was now thirty. Behind him lay what seemed like a whole lifetime of experience—war, travel, work, sport, friendship, love, marriage, fatherhood, and the grueling labors of art.

Hemingway's chief base of operations until 1938 was Key West, but he left it frequently for expeditions elsewhere. In 1930, returning from a hunting trip in Wyoming, he was severely injured in an automobile accident—the first of three serious car crashes he was to be in—and almost lost an arm. In 1932 his third son and last child, Gregory, was born. In 1931 a motion picture version of *A Farewell to Arms* had appeared, with Gary Cooper and Helen Hayes. As a result of it Cooper and Hemingway became warm friends. There was a marked switch at this time in the character of Hemingway's friends. In the twenties they had been mainly writers. In the thirties the writers dropped away and were replaced by movie actors—Marlene Dietrich and, later, Ava Gardner, in addition to Cooper—and by an assortment of nonliterary persons, sailors, sportsmen, and unclassifiable free-lance figures.

A certain prickliness with regard to "intellectuals," that grew more pronounced later on, now appeared in Hemingway. He began to scorn professional and particularly academic critics, and in his own everyday speech affected a down-to-earth, homespun, common-man, anti-educated, pidgin-Indian vocabulary peppered with pungent metaphors from baseball and boxing. This led to a mistaken belief that Hemingway was a boorish plebeian. But his attitude toward culture, literary criticism, and abstract ideas was always two-sided. He corresponded off and on with critics and even college professors to the end of his life, yet harbored a deep distrust of them and their methods. They threatened to deflect him from the purity of his concentration on the physical act, the sensory moment, the communication of which lay at the heart of his writing. He was himself a highly intelligent, widely read man but with a dislike of excessive analysis, of substituting talk for action; or as one of his characters put it, there is "no pleasure in anything if you mouth it up too much."

Two of Hemingway's next three books were works of nonfiction. The first, published in 1932, was *Death in the Afternoon,* an account of bullfighting that was part history and part manual of the sport. Much of the book is in the form of a conversation between Hemingway, appearing in the first person, and an elderly American lady who asks him determined questions and expresses conventional feelings of horror about bullfights. This makes it easy for the author to "explain" the subject without sounding like a formal scholar. And every facet is covered in careful and loving detail: a history of Spanish bullfighting from its classical period of greatness in the eighteenth century to its decline in the present; what makes it a tragedy rather than crude slaughter; minute descriptions of each stage of the bullfight and the whole theory of the slow wearing down of the bull by picadors and banderillos, so that in the end the powerful animal, now trimmed down in strength, and the matador can meet on equal terms; comments on individual matadors, their styles, habits, and degrees of courage; and an extensive glossary of bullfight terms.

In October 1933 another volume of short stories, *Winner Take Nothing,* came out, and that same fall Ernest and Pauline went on safari, hunting big game in East Africa, an expedition that lasted into the spring of 1934. The experience in the African jungle inspired his next book, *Green Hills of Africa,* and two of his celebrated short stories, "The Short Happy Life of Francis Macomber," perhaps his most perfectly designed, flawlessly executed tale, and "The Snows of Kilimanjaro." *Green Hills,* finally published late in 1935, was a straight account of the safari, centering around the stalking of the small-horned kudu and prefaced by a lengthy section in which Hemingway comments on the classic American writers. He has many shrewd things to say about them, acknowledges the influence of Mark Twain and Stephen Crane upon his own work, and declares *Adventures of Huckleberry Finn* to be the greatest single book in our literature. His descriptions of Africa, his evocation of the physical and emotional details of the great hunt, give him another chance to exercise one of his supreme talents as a writer: grappling with nature and sensation at their source.

Like everything else in the country, the books by Hemingway published in the 1930s sold much less briskly than the success of *A Farewell to Arms* had led him to expect. The depression was, of course, chiefly responsible. Key West, along with other American cities, was badly hit by hard times. Breadlines, shantytowns, the corrosive misery of unemployment—all the familiar stigmata of the greatest economic collapse in American history—drew Hemingway momentarily out of his concentration on himself and out of his absorption with the purely personal lives of his characters.

In the middle of the decade he wrote a novel about a free-lance fishing-boat operator named Harry Morgan who, unable to earn a legitimate living because of the depression, is forced to smuggle illegal cargo between Cuba and Florida. During the course of his illicit adventures, he is hounded by the Federal authorities, loses first an arm, then his life while struggling to earn a living for his wife and two daughters and keep them from sinking into the humiliation of the Key West relief rolls. At the end the dying Morgan, named after the famous buccaneer of an earlier day, remarks with his last breath that a man alone has no chance in the world—Hemingway's first step toward collective as contrasted with purely individual action. The novel about Morgan is *To Have and Have Not.* It appeared in 1937 in a first printing of ten thousand copies.

Aside from the depression, the great event of the thirties that aroused Hemingway was the Spanish civil war. In 1931 the bankrupt Spanish monarchy had been overthrown and replaced by a right-wing republican government. The elections of February 1936 brought to power the first liberal-democratic regime in the history of Spain. A few months later, in June, a monarchist-Fascist coalition led by General Francisco Franco revolted against the government. Hitler and Mussolini, the Fascist dictators already established in Germany and Italy, came at once to the aid of Franco. Britain, France, and the United States, however, instead of rallying to their natural allies on the democratic side as might have been expected, imposed an embargo against the legal Spanish government, leaving only Stalin's Russia, for reasons of its own, to provide help. The ferocious civil war that followed aroused passionate emotions all over the world: people were becoming acutely aware of the dangers of Fascism. The war in Spain was the first naked confrontation between the forces that were soon to face each other in the Second World War.

Hemingway's sympathies were with the republicans, or Loyalists as they came to be called. He detested Fascism wherever it appeared, though his love for Spain would probably have drawn him into the upheaval no matter what the contending sides. He spent what money he had and borrowed more to buy ambulances for the government. Anxious to get to Spain as soon as possible, Hemingway accepted an offer from the North American Newspaper Alliance as a foreign correspondent to cover the government's side of the war.

During the three years of the civil war, Hemingway made four separate trips to Spain. He visited the battlefronts, fraternized with the soldiers, stayed for various lengths of time behind the lines in the great cities of Valencia, Barcelona, and Madrid, and renewed his intimate personal contact with Spain. He very much wanted the government to win and was greatly depressed when he saw that it was going to lose. But he was too honest an observer to allow his private sympathies to blind him to the fact that savageries were committed on both sides, that the Loyalists treated their enemies with the same ferocity and brutality as did the Fascists. The capitulation of the government early in 1939 preceded by only a few months the outbreak of the Second World War, but the feelings aroused by the Spanish civil war were in no way dimmed in the minds of Hemingway and his generation by the larger conflict.

As usual, he turned the experience into literature. He wrote a brilliant story, "Old Man at the Bridge," about a small incident in the war that somehow managed to embrace the whole tragedy. He wrote his one play, *The Fifth Column,* about espionage in Madrid. During the siege of Madrid, Franco had four columns of soldiers outside the city and a group of sympathizers and spies within. These were called the "fifth column." Hemingway, in his intense partisanship for the government side, also wrote the commentary for a pro-Loyalist film *The Spanish Earth*. This whole period was climaxed by his longest, most ambitious novel, *For Whom the Bell Tolls*. It appeared late in 1940 and by the spring of 1941 had sold nearly a half million copies. It was the most popular book of Hemingway's career.

The thirties drew to their end, and with them two things came to an end for Hemingway as well, his stay in Key West and his second marriage. He bought a hacienda a few miles outside Havana, Finca Vigia (Lookout Farm), where he was to live for twenty years and would leave, reluctantly, only after the coming of Castro. Cuba was Spanish; it was close to the American mainland; it had spectacular fishing; the cost of living was low—an important consideration for Hemingway who always demanded the best in food, drink, and comfort, and whose personal living expenses, once he began making money, were high.

His second marriage, like his first, had developed serious internal strain. Just as Hemingway's falling in love with Pauline Pfeiffer had been the final dissolving element in his first marriage, so his falling in love with Martha Gellhorn was the final element of dissolution in the second. Miss Gellhorn was a newspaperwoman and a fiction writer. She had traveled widely as a foreign correspondent, had published excellent short stories, and was a brilliantly interesting person. After the divorce from Pauline, Hemingway and she were married in 1940, and it was to her that he dedicated his novel about Spain. They spent part of 1940 and 1941 in the Far East, with Hemingway on assignment from a New York newspaper to report on the growing crisis in the Pacific, soon to be climaxed by the Japanese attack on Pearl Harbor.

Hemingway had fought in the First World War, and had covered practically all the wars since. Military strategy, the psychology of the soldier, the dramatic tensions and pressures that combat imposed upon men, had always fascinated him. It would have been unnatural for him to remain on the sidelines during the Second World War. He was no more able to resist getting into it than he had been able to stay out of the First War. During 1942 and 1943, he was unofficially drafted by the Navy for antisubmarine duty in the Caribbean. He volunteered to chase Nazi U-boats with his own vessel, the *Pilar,* which he had had built for deep-sea fishing and named after the famous character in *For Whom the Bell Tolls.* The work was dangerous. In any outright encounter between the *Pilar* and a submarine, Hemingway would probably have been blown out of the water. His task was to spot enemy

vessels and radio their location back to naval head-
quarters; whether he would engage them in direct combat was his own option. It was ideal work for a man
who craved action but was too old to fit comfortably
into the rigid requirements of an official military
machine.

In 1944, with Allied armies invading both southern
and northern France, Hemingway transferred from
sea to land. Once again he secured a job as war correspondent and soon after D-day found himself in
the front lines. He proceeded not only to cover the
advance of the Allied armies but to take part in it as
an active if free-lance combatant. Before the regular
troops got there, he entered Paris at the head of a small
military party and helped "liberate" the city. At any
rate, he was the first to liberate the Ritz Hotel, his
favorite Parisian hostelry, and there set up his "head-
quarters." The task was made immensely more pleasant
by the discovery that the retreating Germans had not
had time to empty the wine cellars.

For a while he was in trouble with the military authorities, having plainly violated his restricted role as
a reporter. But when this blew over, he was back in the
field again, this time with General Patton's army advancing through eastern France toward Germany. The
unit he was attached to soon found itself functioning,
unofficially, under his command. When its officers were

killed in the Hürtgen Forest, Hemingway took over the tactical operation. By this time he was equipped not only with bottles of bourbon and gin but with pistols and hand grenades, as well as a knowledge of warfare accumulated over almost thirty years of first-hand action and observation.

In 1944 his third marriage, to Martha Gellhorn, broke up. In that year he had met and been attracted to Mary Welsh, still another newspaperwoman. After his third divorce he married her. Mary Welsh became the fourth, and last, Mrs. Ernest Hemingway. This marriage, which endured for seventeen years and ended only with Hemingway's death, was his longest, happiest, and most harmonious.

After the war the Hemingways returned to Cuba where Hemingway began work on his next novel, the highly personal, quasi-autobiographical *Across the River and Into the Trees,* which was finished on the island of Torcello in the lagoon off Venice. It appeared in 1950. Colonel Richard Cantwell, the professional American soldier who is the central figure, was the same age as Hemingway, fifty-one. He, too, had participated in both wars. Like Hemingway he loved Venice, where he had come to spend the last days of his life, and enjoyed food, drink, duck shooting, boxing, and love with equal fervor. Perhaps the resemblance was too close, for the novel suffered from an excessive self-consciousness that made Cantwell's gestures and emotions seem grotesque and parodied. The book may have served as a valuable, even necessary imaginative catharsis for the author, but as a work of art it was Hemingway's most dubious performance.

It was followed almost immediately by *The Old Man and the Sea,* the last of Hemingway's memorable works. The announcement that the book would appear in the September 1, 1952, issue of *Life* aroused uncommon excitement. By this time Hemingway had become the most publicized writer in America. Everything he said and did was avidly recorded by the columnists. His emphatic personality supplied newspaper and magazine editors with endlessly colorful copy.

For once, a story lived up to its advance publicity. *The Old Man and the Sea,* taken on whatever level— as straight narrative of physical action, as Christian parable, as a retelling of an ancient primitive myth— was a powerful short novel. It displayed many of Hemingway's special feelings: his passion for deep-sea fishing, his exquisite sensitivity to the movements of nature, his admiration for courage on a heroic scale raised here once again to an epic pitch, and his absorption with the eternal enigma of man's place in the scheme of things. A week after its magazine appearance the story was issued in book form. Like all of

Hemingway's novels except *Across the River,* it was made into a movie. What with the movie fees and the enormous worldwide sale of his books, he was to leave at his death an estate of well over a million dollars—a sum more often associated with business tycoons than serious and dedicated writers.

In 1953, twenty years after the safari that produced *Green Hills of Africa,* Hemingway, accompanied by Mary, returned once again to big-game hunting, this time in Kenya. The expedition was a disaster. The airplane taking them to Victoria Falls crashed in the jungle. A rescue plane picked them up, and then it, too, crashed. The injuries Hemingway suffered in these two crashes were as serious as any he had sustained in his injury-ridden life. Newspapers all over the world reported him dead. Reading the morbid headlines and the details of his own obituary gave Hemingway a momentary amusement. But it was the only amusing aspect of the months that he spent in an Italian hospital. He returned to Cuba midway through 1954, still not fully recovered.

His distress was lightened somewhat in the fall of 1954 by the announcement that he had won the Nobel Prize for literature. He was not well enough to go to Stockholm and receive the award in person; instead he wrote out a brief acceptance speech, which was delivered for him. The other major American novelist of the century, William Faulkner, had received the Nobel Prize five years earlier when his fame in America was at its lowest point; he was little known to the general reading public and all his major books were out of print. Hemingway was granted the same distinction at the height of his popularity; all his books were in print, and he was even known to millions of persons who had never read any of them.

The universal honor of the Nobel Prize was profoundly gratifying to him, yet it was not without its price. He found himself bombarded by interviewers, tourists, celebrity hunters, cranks, and other persons who for one reason or another hoped to exploit his fame. For a time the Finca Vigia was overrun with them. This greatly exacerbated Hemingway's already edgy nerves. His vanity, as great as any man's, responded to all the adulation, but physically he was in poor condition for it.

Indeed he seemed never really to recover from the mishaps and strains of 1954. He became noticeably more irritable. His moods and temper grew more uncertain, and later in the fifties he began displaying signs of paranoia. Yet he continued to write, live, and travel as ardently as ever. One of his projects was a book of reminiscences about Paris; after his death this was published under the title *A Moveable Feast*. There were rumors that he was working on an immense novel dealing with the Cuban revolution, a *For Whom the Bell Tolls* in a New World setting, and on still another epic concerning the land, air, and sea, of which *The Old Man and the Sea* was a fragment. He was also anxious to bring *Death in the Afternoon* up to date and so kept up with the bullfighting seasons in Spain. He continued to fish, to hunt—mainly from a house he bought in Ketchum, Idaho—to freshen his memories of Europe by brief trips there, and to write.

As had been his habit for many years past, Hemingway continued to do his writing standing up—probably the only author in recorded literature, aside from the great nineteenth-century French novelist Balzac, to do so. Balzac preferred writing at night, dressed in a white nightgown and nightcap, a priestlike uniform for what he regarded as a priestlike office. In Cuba, as often as not, Hemingway would spend the morning standing before his typewriter in shorts. If it was hot, he would be shirtless, wearing nothing above his shorts but a pair of steel-rimmed glasses. He would write through the morning, always being careful to stop at the beginning of a new passage instead of ending with a finished one. He would thus get a fast start the next day. Since his style leaned to economy and sparseness, his daily output was not impressive in terms of number of words. Though he did not produce much quantitatively, he revised what he did write with fanatical zeal, cutting and pruning his first drafts ruthlessly. The old lessons of the Kansas City *Star* were with him still. They were to remain with him to the end.

A dramatic bullfighting episode in Spain lured Hemingway into his last assignment. In the summer of 1959 a competition was arranged between Manuel Ordonez, the reigning matador, and Luis Dominguin, his predecessor who had retired from the ring and was now prevailed upon to return. Hemingway, a close friend of both men, was commissioned by *Life* to cover the contest between them. For weeks he traveled from one dusty bullring to another, following the corridas in which the two performed, absorbing with the intense curiosity of the professional historian the further development of his subject. At last Dominguin was badly gored, bringing the duel to a close, and Hemingway was free to write his articles.

These were published in *Life* under the title "The Dangerous Summer"; they were not vintage Hemingway. The bullfights and the bullfighters were described flaccidly, without the fierce concentration on the significant detail and the unbroken thread of action that distinguished his earlier accounts in *The Sun Also Rises* and in "The Undefeated," the greatest of his bullfighting stories. Hemingway committed the great sin in his own private code as a writer. He allowed feeling—in this case, his personal feeling for the two bullfighters—to stand obtrusively between the reader and the event, romanticizing, blurring, and finally sentimentalizing it.

The strains of living, the heavy pressures to which he had exposed his body and mind, were now beginning to show visibly on Hemingway. His physique, always powerful, had in later years run to fat. His neck was thick, his shoulders and chest massive, sliding down to a large belly, then tapering to a pair of spindly legs. He went on severe diets, lost thirty to forty pounds, and emerged looking ravaged. This ravaged look settled upon him permanently during the late fifties and was accompanied by increasing nervousness, irascibility, and unreasonable outbursts of temper. All these manifestations swelled into full-blown paranoia. He began suspecting his closest friends of wanting to kill him. He imagined himself pursued by Federal agents and surrounded by enemies bent on destroying him. All the care and devotion of his wife and friends could not arrest the progress of this terrifying condition.

In 1960 he gave up his home in Cuba, not because the new regime was forcing him out but because Castro's virulent anti-Americanism made it impossible for him as an American to stay. The process of transplanting himself from Cuba to Idaho was painfully difficult. He had loved Cuba and was deeply attached to the farm where he had lived for twenty years. Giving it up aggravated his nervous malady still further. Various physical infirmities afflicted him—hypertension, partial deafness, hepatitis, a sharp slackening of his sensory responses. After settling in Ketchum, he was twice prevailed upon—each time much against his will—to submit to psychiatric treatment at the Mayo Clinic. The treatments did not help. Back home he had to be forcibly restrained on one occasion from doing violence to himself.

The grim process of degeneration—peculiarly tragic in a man of genius—proceeded remorselessly and could not be checked. In the early morning of July 2, 1961, Hemingway repeated what his father had done nearly twenty-five years before. He shot himself, and brought to a close a life which, for all its superb accomplishments, had become in its final stage too agonizing to endure.

2 THE SUN ALSO RISES

The central theme in Hemingway's longer work is heroism. Contrary to general opinion, his novels are not primarily studies of death or simply researches into the lost generation. They are not just demonstrations of the world's emptiness, of how all things are *nada*. They are essentially portrayals of the hero, the man who by force of some extraordinary quality sets the standard for those around him.

There are two heroes in *The Sun Also Rises:* one open, the other hidden. The open figure is Pedro Romero, the superb young bullfighter, visible to everyone in the sunlit arena as he puts on his matchless exhibitions of skill and courage. Though only nineteen, he is at the height of his power, both as lover and matador. Whatever he does is done supremely. His performance in the bullring, even on a windy day, is first class, sending the spectators into a frenzy of released emotion. In his affair with Lady Brett, he impresses her as being so fine a man that she sends him away because she does not want to ruin him—the first man, in her long career in love, ever to arouse so ideal a sentiment.

Romero's conception of love is an exalting one. He

wants Brett to become a whole woman again, a purifying transformation symbolically represented by his insistence that she allow her bobbed hair to grow long. Equally exalting is his instinctive bravery. When outmatched in his fistfight with Robert Cohn, he refuses to quit, and though knocked down a dozen or more times, keeps getting up and lunging at his tormentor. In the end it is Cohn, sickened by the slaughter, who gives up. Romero's conduct throughout is faultless. He is the born hero.

The hidden hero in the novel is Jake Barnes. On the surface he seems anything but heroic. Emasculated by a wound in the first war, he is cut off from sex, marriage, and fatherhood. An American expatriate living in Paris, he is cut off from his native country: this is beautifully emphasized in the scene where he receives a wedding announcement from Aloysius Kirby in Kansas City, his hometown, and does not have the faintest notion who Kirby is. His friends are rootless cosmopolitans who drift about Europe, restless, bored, without any real occupation. He himself works for the Paris edition of the New York *Herald,* but all he really looks forward to during the year is a two-week vacation that he spends watching the bullfights in Spain. He has a special admiration for bullfighters, whom he regards as the only men who live "all the way up."

Yet this unlikely man, with his discouraging handicap and sterile milieu, is the other hero of the novel—

perhaps even the greater, the ultimate hero. Burdened by a handicap that would crush most men, he bears it stoically. He never tries to sentimentalize it or pretend it does not exist. He is not a soap-opera figure who comes up smiling through his tears. On the contrary, he is almost constantly oppressed by the thought of his injury. He cannot sleep at night while he remembers, against his will, the terrible thing that has happened to him. He can see the humor of the situation, recalling how the Italian colonel praised him with a perfectly straight face for having "given more than your life." But for all the grim comedy and gloomy pathos of his suffering, he has accepted it and gone on functioning as best he can.

If one aspect of heroism is to perform great deeds, like Romero, another—perhaps the more impressive —is to surmount severe difficulties through a constant exercise of self-disciplining willpower. Jake manages to perform all the functions possible to him: he prays, labors, suffers, helps, loves with passionate faithful emotion, and goes through acts of purgation. For those readers who enjoy quasi-cabalistic pursuits, the biblical character of all this might be suggested by his first name. The first, fourth, and fifth letters of Jacob spell Job, while the second and third letters might stand for After Christ. As a Catholic, he is a Job who appears after Christ.

His efforts are all in the direction of life and the

heightening of his human faculties. He cannot be a bullfighter himself, but he can be the next best thing, an aficionado, who understands bullfighting thoroughly and reacts to it with the exquisite sensitivity of a connoisseur. *Aficion,* we are told, means passion; an aficionado is one who is passionate about bullfights. Jake has this kind of passion, the passion of knowledge rather than the passion of the act itself, the emotion of the spectator instead of the participant. This passion may be secondary and derivative, but it is wholly authentic, meaningful, and pure, and something that Jake had to acquire through persistent effort. The Spaniards regard this as almost nonexistent in Americans. Montoya, the hotelkeeper in Pamplona who allows only aficionados to stay in his hotel during the festival of San Fermin, expresses his surprise that Jake is an American. Jake is the only American Montoya and his friends have ever met who has *aficion*. Montoya finds this so impressive that he relaxes his own strict house rule and allows Jake to bring his plainly non-aficionado friends to the hotel.

Jake is also the connecting link in all the human relationships of the novel. Without him many of these could never have been established, and others would have broken down. He is the only person who can get along with Robert Cohn. He introduces Cohn to his circle of friends and manages to keep him there far longer than he could have remained on his own. It is Jake who introduces Lady Brett to Romero, thus initiating him into the necessary contact with worldly corruption and providing Brett with her first experience in moral purity. This rouses her to her one definitive moral act: as she sends Romero away, she observes that she is no longer capable of doing good, but she can still refrain from doing evil; no higher exaltation is open to her bruised nature.

Jake is the buffer among his friends, the steer who quiets the angry bulls. He is also a kind of confessor to whom they all come with their troubles. Out of the resources of his own self, he supplies the human lubricant that makes their society possible. He rescues Brett, befriends Cohn, listens patiently to Harvey Stone, accompanies Bill, calms Mike, appreciates Count Mippipopolous, attracts Harris, and admires Romero for the right reasons. He links Robert Cohn, a Jew, to the Christian world. Through his contact with Montoya and Romero, he is the liaison between his non-Spanish friends and the Spaniards. Without being able to live wholly himself, he is a catalytic agent who releases life in others.

In Pamplona he commutes between the cathedral and the wine-cellar, thus connecting Catholicism and paganism. Ultimately he is the link between city and country, urban and rural society, man and nature. The second of the novel's two epigraphs, from Ecclesiastes, dramatizes the idea that generations of men come and go but "the earth abideth forever." It is to the earth that Jake deliberately returns each year, there to refresh himself at the source of the one enduring reality in Hemingway's universe. There is the sun which also rises and the earth which always abides—beyond them, nothing. Before the fiesta begins, Jake and Bill go into the hills above Burguete, deep in the Spanish countryside. They stay at a little rural inn and go trout fishing in the Irate river. Here Jake is lifted out of the difficulties and ambiguities that beset him in Paris and Pamplona. An emotional serenity sets in. He feels liberated, however briefly. Brett, Robert Cohn, and their messy lives are far away. Jake eats and drinks well, sleeps deeply, fishes and reads undisturbed, and makes friends directly and simply with the Englishman Harris. Then the inevitable telegram comes from Pamplona, summoning him back to civilization and its spiritual confusions.

This return to nature lends itself to exaggerated interpretations. It has been called Hemingway's Garden of Eden myth or an infantile womb regression where the stricken soul wishes to slide back from adult responsibilities or the quiet Spenserian bower where a man retreats to recover from some psychic wound. Or it has been regarded as an escape from real life and the real world, in support of the theory that Hemingway is really an adolescent writer who never managed to attain maturity. These and other forms of critical inflation—some footling, some highly ingenious—have been aroused by Hemingway's attitude toward nature.

The refusal to take this attitude for what it is, at face value and in the most forthright way, has been astonishing. His nature is simply nature—woods, streams, unspoiled sunlight—a delight to experience and to re-create senses and spirit in. The country is as much a part of the real world as the city, and to Hemingway, remembering the pleasures of his boyhood, a source of special power. He is not a Rousseau, the eighteenth-century French philosopher who urged mankind to return to the soil, or a Thoreau, withdrawing from the human world to sit on a tree stump and contemplate natural phenomena, or a Steinbeck, yearning for a primitive paradise. To Hemingway human society is the arena of experience; the woods, the place of restoration.* Neither is complete without

---

* *Only in Hemingway's last story,* The Old Man and the Sea, *is this process reversed. Santiago, the aged Cuban fisherman, goes forth onto the lonely sea for his great adventure and comes back to his village for rest and recuperation after it is over. His extreme old age, with its implication of detachment from the human norm, gives this reversal its dramatic plausibility.*

the other. Nor does one exist on a higher level of moral or spiritual excellence than the other, nor is either an "escape."

They have different qualities and different functions, largely complementary. Perhaps the greatest difference in quality is the transience of society and the permanence of nature, but even this does not make the second "preferable" to the first. Jake moves back and forth between society and nature easily. When the summons comes from the human world, he answers it without hesitation. He and Bill bid Harris good-bye and return to Pamplona, to the half-Christian, half-pagan fiesta of San Fermin with its saints, bullfights, and *riau-riau* dancers, to what Bill, in one of the novel's most compelling phrases, calls "the wonderful nightmare."

A good deal of the book is taken up with eating and drinking. As the first-person narrator, Jake is in the middle of this, too, as he is of everything else. Here, too, he practises another of his humanizing functions. He discriminates in his choice of food and wine as carefully as in his relationship with people. He does not wish just to fill his stomach and quench his thirst. He wants to enjoy what he eats, to savor it, and thus heighten his sense of selective pleasure in the act that consumes so much of the human day. Hemingway's pages are dotted with descriptions of restaurants, bars, menus, and wine lists. They are there to demonstrate that even in the simple elementary actions of life one can proceed with fineness and delicacy of perception. Living or trying to live with supreme skill is a moral action, and the moral choice lies between doing something indifferently or doing it well. Hemingway absorbed these ideas from the work of an earlier writer whom he greatly admired, Joseph Conrad, who in his own way gave skill an ethical stature. To Conrad a seaman who did his job ably was a far more admirable moral agent than, for example, the social reformer who sought to remake the world on abstract principles.

In the daily struggle to maintain himself Jake succeeds to a remarkable degree, but never altogether. This is beyond him because ultimately there is nothing he can do about his disability. He loves Brett abidingly, and she him, but their love can never be consummated. Moreover, he finds himself in the painful situation of introducing her to men who later become her lovers, perhaps as unconscious substitutes for himself. But even aside from this, he has normal human shortcomings. His friendship with Cohn progresses to a point; when strain develops, he breaks it off. He joins in the baiting of Cohn, though ashamed of himself afterward. Jake is a Catholic and gets a true religious feeling on the rare occasions when he attends

Mass, yet he ignores the acts required of him by the Church and considers himself a bad Catholic. He tries to hold his group of friends together in Pamplona but fails, and pays a heavy price for the failure in the rupture with Montoya. Between aspiration and achievement, there is always a gap that Jake strains to bridge without ever quite succeeding. His heroism, unlike Romero's, is not that of consummation but of effort. Both men illustrate Hemingway's celebrated definition of courage as grace under pressure. Jake, however, endures by far the greater pressure, so that the relative grace with which he bears himself is a more striking though less visible phenomenon than Romero's.

All this rests upon Jake's ruthless honesty. He dare not fool himself by pretending that things are other than they are. He dare not daydream or sentimentalize either his own situation or the character of his friends. He bluntly describes Brett as a drunk. He is perfectly aware that Cohn is an aggrieved adolescent with a gnawing inferiority complex and that Mike Campbell is an emotional as well as a financial bankrupt. He knows that things will never get any better, and that if he himself had not been wounded in the war, he still would have been hurt—as all the others have been hurt—in some other way.

The others give way to illusions that Jake cannot

afford and to which he does not succumb. In the final exchange of the novel Brett, rescued once again by Jake, says to him, "We could have had such a damn good time together," referring of course to how it might have been had he not been wounded. Jake replies wryly, "Isn't it pretty to think so," and the book ends on this highly realistic note. However tempted, Jake will not permit himself to believe that life is anything but harsh and irremediable. He will not engage in idle soothing fancies of what might have been. If he did, everything would get out of control, and he would drown in self-dramatization and self-pity. The hard truth is all that can save him. He clings to it with justifiable desperation, and not even the ravishing Brett, achingly in love with her as he is, can sway him from it. Romero does not quail before the lunging horns of the bulls or before Cohn's educated fists. Jake does not flinch before his painful lot. The bullfighter is the universal hero, recognizable at all times and places. In Jake, Hemingway has created a special type of modern hero, the hero who functions inside the façade of the antihero. It is hard to say which is the more compelling and persuasive, the performance or the disguise.

The last words of the novel are Jake's astringent comment to Brett. Its first words, indeed its first two chapters, deal with Robert Cohn, in every respect

Jake's foil. On the surface he has every advantage. He is good looking, independently rich, and attractive to women. Educated at the best schools, he has written one successful book and is at work on another. He is a champion boxer and trained athlete. Nothing in the world seems beyond his reach. Yet beneath the surface he is soft, vain, and emotionally mushy. Badly spoiled by the generosities that nature and fortune have heaped upon him, he expects all his wishes to be gratified and turns childishly sullen when they are not. He believes naïvely in the absolute, in the old liberal dream that all things are attainable, that nothing is beyond human reach. In this he is as invincibly immature as Jake, who accepts the finiteness of things, is manifestly wise. In this sense Cohn does not know the score, the cosmic score as Hemingway reads it, and acts as a principle of dissolution among those who do.

Unable to accept the world as it is, Cohn with obstinate romanticism is forever breathing his own emotions into others. A casual weekend with Brett convinces him that she must be in love with him, despite all her assertions to the contrary. He stubbornly clings to this conviction, absorbs countless snubs and humiliations while defending it, and does not, reluctantly, give up until struck a final series of sledgehammer blows. Along with his drive for success, he also has a will to failure, and along with his facility, pugilistic and otherwise, for inflicting pain on others, takes a masochistic pleasure in absorbing pain himself. The scene in the Paris café where Frances heaps abuse upon him while he sits unretaliating establishes his character. Jake, witness to the episode, is sickened by it and leaves in the middle.

Cohn's erratic responses give Hemingway an opportunity to expound his belief in the individual will. Anything can be borne if one goes into training for it. Jake has been forced into perpetual training, and he emerges in the novel as the supreme example of the spiritual athlete. Cohn's training has been only in the ring. He is very nice, as Jake says, and a good tennis friend, but whether he will ever make it otherwise—that is, develop the will to endure the idea that human objectives are only partly attainable—remains uncertain. He is an unfinished man, a note struck in the novel's opening paragraph when Jake remarks, "I never met any one of his class at Princeton who remembered him."

The other characters share with Jake his stoic knowledge of the universe but share with Cohn a common failure of the will. Brett knows what it is all about but finds the knowledge too painful to bear and sinks into the endless oblivion of unsatisfying and impermanent sex. Mike's escape is the bottle. Bill shields himself behind a screen of bitter wisecracks. Count Mippipopolous—a true adventurer in his youth—now in middle age seeks refuge in a perpetual champagne party that goes on day and night, gathering up whoever is around as it moves along. These characters oscillate between the two extremes of Cohn and Jake. Appropriately it is Cohn's voice we hear at the beginning of the novel and Jake's at the end.

The story is divided into three parts, in a sequence that in itself reveals the viewpoint of the novel. Part one, Paris, is static: the characters are introduced and shown living their routine lives. Part two, Pamplona, is climax: the bullfights and other excitements of the festival lift the cast out of their ordinary existence to a supercharged level.* Part three is again static anticlimax: with the fiesta over, everyone drifts back to France, lapsing back into the routine in which they were seen at the start. The climactic feature of life is that it is anticlimactic, the very circumstance that Jake grapples with so tenaciously. The structure of the book, which begins and ends with anticlimax, reflects this theme with ruthless exactitude. At the same time

---

* *The town fathers of Pamplona were so moved by his tribute to their city that a few years after his death they named a street "Paseo Hemingway," in honor of the writer who had immortalized Pamplona in his greatest work.*

it underlines the epigraph from Ecclesiastes: "All the rivers run into the sea; yet the sea is not full; unto the place from whence the rivers come, thither they return again." Men, like the other phenomena of earth, are caught up in the cycle of perpetual recurrence.

The problem for the men and women in *The Sun Also Rises*—Romero excepted—is not how to succeed but how to survive. The style of the novel illuminates that problem as much as its structure catches the essential life rhythm of the characters. Hemingway's style is perhaps the best-known and certainly the most widely advertised aspect of his work. His stripped vocabulary, simple sentences, monosyllabic diction, repetitive sequences, stress on nouns and verbs and avoidance of adjectives and adverbs, and deliberate hostility to any kind of ornamental rhetoric or overt commentary have been admired, imitated, and caricatured in about equal measure. The influence of this style upon the writers of the mid-twentieth century has been enormous, covering a whole range from J. D. Salinger to Dashiell Hammett, Raymond Chandler, and the purveyors of hard-boiled detective stories in *Black Mask* magazine. Hemingway sought to restore vernacular English as a literary medium, purge the language of Melville's purple prose and Henry James's labyrinthine subtleties, and get back to the colloquial simplicity of Mark Twain. Hemingway approved of Rimbaud's famous cry, "Let us seize rhetoric by the throat and strangle it."

He strove to secure the maximum effect through the minimum means, to see how much he could express in the fewest possible words. He was constantly testing his language to see how large a weight of thought and emotion it could carry, not by dissipating these over a diffuse arena of words but by concentrating, even telescoping them in the tightest possible space. In the same way he was always gauging how much pressure each character could stand in the test of individual survival.

The very act of paring language down to the absolute essentials suggests and supports the process by which men prepare for survival. They can afford nothing extra, no superfluous paraphernalia, no excess baggage. They must travel light. They, too, must strip down to the bare minimum. Again Jake is the supreme example. He must free his mind of all illusions and needless preoccupations, and be on guard against the invasion of complicating, trouble-making thoughts and memories. This is especially difficult at night, when he lies in bed vainly trying to fall asleep. Then, against his will, the intruders come, fasten themselves upon him, fill his head with a "wheeling sensation," and remind him of the wretchedness of his plight. "It is awfully easy to be hard-boiled about everything in the daytime," he thinks, "but at night it is another thing."

He struggles to check the thoughts whirling about in him. In a key statement midway through the book, he reflects, "I did not care what it was all about. All I wanted to know was how to live in it." The substitution of *how* for *what*—action for meaning—was perhaps the way to keep things under control. Live, act, do, with a minimum of reflection and analysis. Again the drive to strip existence to its working essence. "Maybe," continues Jake, "if you found out how to live in it you learned from that what it was all about." The philosophical meaning of life could be reached only through the back door of action, if at all. And if it cannot be reached, it may be dispensed with.

If the moment of action can be described truly— to borrow one of Hemingway's favorite abverbs—then the emotion it contains will be automatically released. The emotion is concealed in the action, just as the *what* is concealed in the *how*. Hemingway's art consists of packing as much feeling and thought as he can into the sensory act. He does so partly because thought, if approached directly in art and ladled straight out to the reader, becomes propaganda; and feeling, if too directly approached, becomes sentimentality. But he has another reason: the process of concentration and condensation for the writer is the equivalent of the same process undertaken by his characters for the sake of their own human continuation. Underaccenting does not destroy or eliminate meaning, but only leaves it implied. By leaving it implied rather than stated, a larger amount of meaning can be contained in a smaller space. Proper leverage can lift unexpectedly heavy weights, and traveling light does not mean traveling empty; it means traveling without anything superfluous. The superfluous is as much an emotional drain on Jake as it is an aesthetic and verbal drain on Hemingway's lean, trained prose. His famous style is there not for its own sake, or for the greater glory of the author, but as the necessary instrument for the kind of story being told and the particular vision of human existence being conveyed.

Nowhere is Hemingway more clearly revealed as an American than in his preoccupation with the how of living. Pragmatism, formulated by William James, has been the one original American philosophy, and its central question about the reality of any experience, Does it work? has also been the central question of American history from the early days of the geographic frontier to the present age of the technological. Hemingway is the supreme technician among

American writers, and his heroes are supremely concerned with the technique of whatever they are doing. Whatever their activity—whether fishing in "Big Two-Hearted River" and *The Old Man and the Sea,* boxing in "Fifty Grand," bullfighting in "The Undefeated," hunting in "The Short Happy Life of Francis Macomber," soldiering in *For Whom the Bell Tolls* and *Across the River and Into the Trees,* or living, as in Jake's case, with as much grace as possible from day to day—the question of technique is decisive.

Ethics, a branch of philosophy with which James was not primarily concerned, is subordinate to method. Morality in Hemingway, whenever he ventures to define it directly, is reduced to a matter of mood. On one of his sleepless nights, Jake tries to define morality, but finds it too confusing and gives up. This does not mean that Hemingway—or William James—is neutral on the subject. Hemingway is intensely concerned with moral discriminations, but like questions of metaphysics, the what of things, these are implied in the doing process. And this process is always approached in a spirit of pragmatism. Skill, rather than goodness or badness, is Hemingway's main interest. An act well done creates its own goodness. Something supremely well done carries with it its own ecstasy and its own supreme morality. The right action, not the right thought, is the ultimate healer. This is implicit in the advice given to Nick Adams in "The Killers": "You'd better not think about it."

We are not a nation of Platonists. The world of the senses, which Plato so distrusted, intoxicates us, and it is this world that Hemingway addressed himself to and mastered. He had a well-publicized disdain of critics, college professors, and intellectuals. Despite his own wide reading in several foreign languages, he never wanted to be taken for a "cultured" man; sometimes he assumed a pidgin-Indian vocabulary during interviews to disguise himself still further. Though Hemingway spent much of his adult life abroad and was a leading expatriate of the twenties, he never for a moment ceased being an American writer, pursuing and expressing the chief direction of the American mind.

The Sun Also Rises is filled with incidental riches. The characters are brought immediately into focus with a series of quick revealing details. Lady Brett is first seen defeminized, with a group of homosexuals; her hair is cropped and brushed back like a boy's. She is forever bathing and washing herself, speaks in unfinished sentences, and tries in vain to feel an emotion in church. Cohn compares her to Circe turning men into swine, but though he is jeered at for the image, the comparison is valid. Cohn himself is nearsighted, never gets drunk, is bored by the bullfights, and falls asleep at crucial moments, notably at the height of the Dionysian revels in Pamplona. Jake is linked with empty barges on the Seine, drained wine glasses, stuffed dogs, and steers; he has a genius for getting along with everyone, from Parisian prostitutes, Basque peasants, and long-distance bicycle riders to upper-class English; he knows the differences between French and Spanish waiters, can hold forth intelligently on the art of tipping, and is exquisitely responsive to changes of landscape. Bill, a word lover, runs off on coruscating dashes with words that catch his fancy: his virtuoso performances with "utilize" and "irony and pity" are memorable little tours de force.

Hemingway is seldom associated with humor or lightness of touch, yet the novel is peppered with witty moments: the discussion of W. H. Hudson and his book *The Purple Land* in Chapter Three, or Jake reading A. E. W. Mason, a now-forgotten romantic novelist, during the fishing expedition; Jake's comment about the newspaper business that it is "an important part of the ethics that you should never seem to be working"; the biting description of Frances Kline as "a very tall girl who walked with a great deal of movement"; Jake's concierge whose opinions vary according to the size of the tip; the religious dining-car episode on the train to Biarritz; Bill on the assorted subjects of his face, American expatriates, Henry James, and Abraham Lincoln; Mike relating the two ways in which he went bankrupt, "Gradually and then suddenly"; Brett remarking that she has the wrong type of face for churchgoing; Jake's satire on the French and money, and his spoofing of the Spanish language as he enters Brett's hotel in Madrid. The book also has its share of pithy social observations. Here is one: "The room was in that disorder produced only by those who have always had servants." Neither Henry James nor F. Scott Fitzgerald, acknowledged masters in this line, ever did better than that.

The Sun Also Rises may well be Hemingway's masterpiece, but it has at least one jarring note. A streak of nastiness runs through it, an element that surfaces from time to time in Hemingway's other work. An immediate sign of this is the Jew-baiting of Cohn. Mike is the most vicious in this respect, but Bill joins in, too, as does Jake. References are made to Cohn's "Jewish superiority," to his pushiness, and even to his nose, which was improved by being flattened in the ring. Watching Cohn gazing at Brett, the Jew coveting the Christian lady, Jake thinks, "He looked a great deal as his compatriot must have looked when he saw the promised land." No one can quarrel with Hemingway's intention in making Cohn a Jew in the first place; he wished to give him from the start a built-in sense of uncertainty and inferiority. And it is, after all, his fictional characters and not he who direct their barbs at Cohn. But the exaggerated and unflattering allusions to the state of being Jewish clearly exceed what the revelation of their social attitudes would normally demand.

Hemingway was not anti-Semitic, as Ezra Pound was throughout his career and T. S. Eliot was during the early stage of his. But something moved him to drive the anti-Semitism of his characters beyond the limits required by the novel. The same is true of the anti-Negro slurs, indulged in chiefly by Bill. The Negroes, referred to unfailingly as "niggers," are not like Conrad's Nigger of the *Narcissus:* Conrad's figure was a powerful personality, a center of demoniac strength; Bill's references are of no consequence to the story. Here, too, it is not so much the author's racial opinions that are being exposed but a latent defect of temperament, a vein of suspiciousness and hostility, that finds indirect expression in the excessive and at times needless abuse of individual ethnic groups. Hemingway's brother remembered how quick

Ernest was to take offense, how slow to forgive, and how ruthlessly he would ostracize any of his friends who he fancied had "crossed" him. This was to grow into the uncontrollable paranoia of his last months.

A more persistent indication of the same prickly quality is the tendency of his characters to draw themselves into cultist enclaves. The "in" group, Jake and his circle in *The Sun Also Rises,* sets up rigorous tests for the admission of newcomers, as arbitrary as any established by country clubs, college fraternities, or exclusive societies anywhere. Count Mippipopolous passes the test and is admitted because of his arrow wounds and his knowing, to Brett's satisfaction, what life is all about. Cohn does not pass the test, despite Jake's friendly sponsorship, and is thereupon cast into outer darkness. Insiders and outsiders, those in the know and those in the dark, split Hemingway's figures into inexorable categories.

Again the motivation is compelling. If the world is without divinity or ultimate purpose, human beings must build for themselves their own stockades, with high fences to keep out both the bleak universe and those who do not know how to survive in it. One ventures out into the surrounding dark from time to time to challenge death, as a means of testing and strengthening one's nerves and powers of endurance, only to withdraw into what is, hopefully, the reassuring protection of the interior. Persons like Cohn, who mess things up emotionally, have to be expelled as a simple matter of self-preservation.

The psychology of inclusion and exclusion carries within it, however, its own endemic disease: those excluded tend to be regarded not simply as dangerous but as members of an inferior species, and the emotional attitude of the insiders alters, often by imperceptible degrees, from dispassionate indifference to hostility and contempt. Traces of this are evident in the treatment of Cohn. They become more visible in the later work. In Hemingway's last full-length novel, *Across the River and Into the Trees,* they are rampant. Colonel Cantwell forms instant secret groups with the few people he likes to keep out the many he dislikes. His contempt for the Milan profiteers in Venice—he himself is a foreigner who has become more Venetian than the Venetians—provides one of the less agreeable passages in Hemingway. It is a symptom of the emotional imbalance that distorts the whole frame of the novel.

This difficulty aside, and it is only a muffled note in the work of the twenties, *The Sun Also Rises* emerges as a remarkable achievement. It is the definitive account of the expatriate era. As a mood piece, it catches the lost generation in a moment of feverish luminosity. It is an exquisitely verbalized tone poem. It presents within its small realized context the universal process by which human beings struggle to achieve their humanity against formidable obstacles. And in Jake it has created a figure complex enough to bear, without absurdity or sentimentality, the pressure of his own submerged heroism.

3 A FAREWELL TO ARMS

Like *The Sun Also Rises, A Farewell to Arms* is about a love affair between an American and an English-woman. Only this time it is consummated. Frederic Henry and Catherine Barkley are the lovers in question and their affair takes place during the First World War. The time is some years before the events of *The Sun Also Rises,* though *A Farewell to Arms* was written later. The title has a double reference. Lieutenant Henry deserts from the Italian army in which he enlisted as a medical corpsman; he makes, as he says, his own separate peace while the war is still on. There is another farewell to arms in the story: as Catherine dies in childbirth at the end, a farewell is bade to the arms of lovers and of love.

War and love supply the novel with its counter-point. Hemingway deliberately wrote it on the plan of *Romeo and Juliet*. The feud of the Montagues and Capulets is a form of war, with violence and blood-shed and innocent victims. Romeo and Juliet both die;

though Frederic, unlike Catherine, does not die in the physical sense, he suffers an emotional death. The priest in *A Farewell to Arms* is as important as the priest in Shakespeare's play. The Mercutio figure is Rinaldi, skeptical about the war as Mercutio is about the feud, just as bitterly cynical, and just as steadfast in friendship. Frederic, like Romeo, progresses from sex to love, from surface attachment to abiding passion. With a little ingenuity, analogies can also be seen among the minor characters in the two works. The play is divided into five acts, the novel into five parts, and both take place in Italy.

Along with these close similarities, there is one significant difference. Romeo and Juliet are the victims of the family feud, and die because of it. Catherine's death, however, is a biological accident, having nothing to do with the war. The interrelated, cause-and-effect universe of Shakespeare has been replaced, in Hemingway, by a world where disasters are senseless and irrelevant. Hemingway gives special emphasis to this element of blind, purposeless accident. Not only in love, but on the battlefield, where survival has always been a matter of luck, Hemingway dramatizes the role of chance. A few inches closer and the mortar shell that shattered Lieutenant Henry's knee would have killed him as it did the man next to him.

The effect of an accidental universe is to break

everything up into isolated units. Since the connections between these units are either haphazard or non-existent, they are surrounded by blank spaces. The love affair of Romeo and Juliet takes place against a dense background of friends, relatives, parents, servants, messengers, suitors, priests, and heads of state. The love affair of Frederic and Catherine takes place only against the faceless, impersonal landscape of modern war, with hardly anyone around. In its last stages, in Switzerland, where they come as refugees and know absolutely nobody, it exists in total isolation. This lends the note of poignancy and even desperation to their feelings, especially Catherine's, which is the peculiar product of aloneness. The deaths of Romeo and Juliet lead to the ending of the feud—the play has its causality and continuity at the end as at the beginning. Catherine's death leads nowhere. The war still goes on, and Frederic is about where he was when he met her. Both works are in this respect perfect illustrations of how an author's metaphysics shapes his art.

The isolation of Hemingway's lovers is heightened by their being torn away from their origins. Like Jake, Frederic is a long way from America and only tenuously connected with it. Though English, Catherine has no ties left with England. There is no question at any time of returning to their own countries. As outsiders in Italy, their position is more emotionally neutral than the natives'. Frederic makes friends among the Italians, serves in the Italian army, is wounded for the Italian cause, yet drifts through these experiences with a curious kind of detachment, always outside them even as a participant. All his stored-up, unused emotional energy is turned toward Catherine, and hers toward him. The fierceness of their love, the exaggerated intensity of their feelings, are as much a product of their separation from society as of any unusual capacity for passion in themselves.

Society appears very little in Hemingway's work. His absorption in society is slight; his suspicion, even hostility to it, marked. His characters are separated from it, like those of his early master Joseph Conrad. Lord Jim in his Malay refuge, Marlow in the heart of Africa, Adolf Verloc in the London underground, Razumov among the exiled Russian revolutionaries in Switzerland are as intensely alone, as removed from social sanctions and social ties, as the aged fisherman in *The Old Man and the Sea* or the young lovers in *A Farewell to Arms*. This is the essence of the expatriate experience for Hemingway. It is a flight from organized society, from which, in its American form, Hemingway was as alienated as Krebs in his early story "Soldier's Home." The expatriate can live in another country for years, as Conrad did in England or

Hemingway in France, without ever being obliged to establish new social connections—a far easier task, obviously, in a foreign country than in one's own.

Everything in *A Farewell to Arms* is built around the lovers, as though the cruel war, the empty cosmos, and the lost homeland can be redeemed by the depth of their feelings for one another. It would take an extraordinary couple to bear up under all this strain and shoulder so much responsibility. Frederic and Catherine are not equal to it; perhaps no single pair of lovers could be—not even Vronsky and Anna Karenina, the great figures in Tolstoy's novel *Anna Karenina*, for all their superior vitality and the added richness of character which was the result of being past their first youth. Tolstoy, at any rate, does not expect them to carry the entire weight of his great novel; he has a rich supporting cast.

A supporting cast, however, does not suit Hemingway's purposes. The note of isolation that he wishes to strike is better served by stripping his lovers of everything and everyone but themselves. This may make matters more difficult for his novel but is truer to his conception of things. In line with this conception his cities, for example, are singularly uncrowded. London in the novels of Dickens and Thackeray is a teeming place, as are Moscow in Tolstoy, Paris in Balzac, St. Petersburg in Dostoevsky, and Dublin in

Joyce. But Paris, Madrid, and Venice in Hemingway's work seem to have nobody in them except the handful of main characters.

Of the two chief figures in *A Farewell to Arms,* Catherine is the less convincing. The difficulty is that she has nothing to do in the story except be in love with Frederic. He, however, has exciting experiences outside the orbit of love. He goes off to the war from time to time, is wounded, and manages a thrilling escape from the Italian army when the carabinieri are about to shoot him during the retreat from Caporetto. He has stimulating conversations with Rinaldi, Count Greffi, and the priest. All this gives his personality a chance to breathe more expansively and to grow in the reader's imagination. In any case, his intimate presence is established at once by the fact that he is the first-person narrator. His reflections and comments, brief as they are, are revealed to us directly. When early in their relationship Catherine begs him to say he loves her, he says so readily while notifying us at the same time that he is lying. In the creation of character the advantage to the author of such immediate communication is overwhelming.

The disadvantage of using a first-person narrator is that it restricts all the other figures to his presence. If he is not around, they cannot be. What they say and do is limited by and therefore dependent upon his witnessing it. In a sense they exist only so far as he, by his movements and testimony, allows them to. Catherine suffers especially from this restrictiveness. She is seen only through Frederic's eye and must live her whole life in the novel within that single focus. Since his interest in her is amatory, she appears only as a love object. Whatever qualities or resources she may have of any other kind are blanked out in advance. The result is a character too limited to bear the emotional demands made upon her.

Another limitation in the portrayal of Catherine is that she is made to fall so terrifyingly and clingingly in love with Frederic, yielding herself so utterly to him, that she virtually abandons her own personality in the process and becomes a leechlike shadow of his. Her single, fixed role as a clinging vine denies her the opportunity for experience and compels her to equate her relationship to Frederic with the whole of life. She tries to assure him (when she becomes pregnant) that neither she nor the baby will be any trouble to him. At an early point her dialogue consists of remarks like these: "I'll say just what you wish and I'll do what you wish and then you will never want any other girls, will you?" "I'll do what you want and say what you want and then I'll be a great success, won't I?" "I want what you want. There isn't any me any more. Just what you want!" To such embarrassing state-

ments, there is not very much he can say. He is reduced to the brief laconic reply: "Yes." Or: "You're
so lovely." Or: "You sweet."

Her overstatements and his countering understate-
ments produce vacuums in their conversation. Many
of these are filled with self-praise. "We are splendid
people," she exclaims. Both of the lovers indulge
in such self-exaltation. They are forever calling one
another brave, lovely, and splendid. The more isolated
they become, the more they are thrown into each
other's company, the more significance they read into
their own natures as people in love and into the nature
of their relationship. Frederic, who does what thinking is done for both of them, has his two celebrated
little outbursts on their position in the world. In one
he argues that the good, the gentle, and the brave—
among whom he counts himself and Catherine—are
sure to be killed by the hostile universe before ordinary
people will be. In the other, while watching ants on a
burning log, he compares them to humanity. He reflects that he can play the role of God by lifting the
log off the fire and throwing it where the ants can get
off. But all he does is empty a cup of water on the
log, which only steams the ants.

The result of these reflections is to inflate the lovers
above the ordinary. They are endowed with the special
virtues of courage, gentleness, and goodness that put

them in a select class beyond the usual run of mortals. Frederic can even imagine himself metaphorically in the place of a supreme power, with the same option of life and death over human beings as men have over ants. As God with regard to men, he chooses to do nothing. As a man with regard to ants, he goes about his own business, emptying the cup of water in order to fill it with whiskey. As a parable, the anecdote of the ants sums up aptly Hemingway's view of the indifferent universe in which human beings have no more privileged place than ants.

But as Frederic's unconscious effort to invest himself with powers larger than life, it is less persuasive. He is an exceptional man in one great respect—coolness under physical pressure, as proven in his sensational escape from his would-be army executioners and in the equally sensational voyage across Lake Maggiore. This is hardly enough to justify the large emotional and spiritual qualities which he ascribes to himself and Catherine. To prove oneself in action is one thing; to simply assert one's superiority is another. There is an excess of assertion over action in their relationship. If their assertions were compelling or their conversation fascinating, the imbalance might have been corrected. Neither is the case, and the gap between the claims the lovers make for themselves and the demonstrated reality persists.

Their love affair as such is perfectly convincing. It generates all the poignancy Hemingway wishes it to have. It develops credibly beyond the sexual to that deeper feeling which causes the lovers to look upon it as a true marriage. But it becomes tedious to the reader. The amorous small talk grows increasingly specialized. As the lovers find it more interesting, the reader finds it more boring. Their natures are neither rich enough nor nuanced enough to carry the whole emotional burden; the novel suffers its major setback in the disproportion between their feelings and their revealed characters. They are, of course, lovers in the romantic tradition, giving up the world for the sake of their love. But this very defiance is what starves it by turning it inward upon themselves and depriving it of fertilizing social roots.

Hemingway tries to widen the scope of the love affair by shifting its locale as much as possible. His lovers meet in a village just behind the lines, move from there to a hospital in Milan, then to Stresa, then to Switzerland. The stay in Switzerland is divided between the mountains above Montreux and Lausanne. The changes in scenery freshen the emotional atmosphere, which tends to be overheated and enclosed, and give the lovers something to do besides gaze into each other's eyes. They are carried out of themselves, away from their excessive concentration on each other. Their moving about as much as they do is a relief to the reader as well as to themselves.

In other respects the novel carries out its intentions with margin to spare. Everything having to do with the war—the other half of *A Farewell to Arms*— is handled with supreme skill. The brief opening chapter—its five paragraphs a miniature replica of the novel's five parts—is a model of its kind. The first two paragraphs and half of the third deal with summer: the season is rich and fertile, and by way of response, the war goes well; the water in the streams is clear blue; the orchards are crowded with fruit trees; the nights are cool. Even the big guns drawn by ivy-covered tractors are camouflaged by green branches and seem like objects in a flowering landscape.

Midway through paragraph three the season changes to autumn, and the rain begins, the rain that serves throughout the novel as a symbol of disaster. Rain makes Catherine morbid; she has a recurrent dream in which she sees herself dead in the rain. In modern literature rain is usually a fructifying element, as in T. S. Eliot's *The Waste Land,* but Hemingway, who disliked Eliot, reverses the symbol, embedding it in gloom, dampness, mud, chill, and the miseries of war.

The trees are now bare; the vineyards stripped; and

"all the country wet and brown and dead with the autumn." The paragraph closes with the vivid, grotesque, unnatural image of the soldiers, keeping their cartridge boxes dry inside their coats, looking "as though they were six months gone with child." The fourth paragraph satirically describes the visits to the front by the undersized Italian king. He came out "every day to see how things were going, and things went very badly." This prepares the way for the briefest of the five paragraphs, the two-sentence fifth, which announces the coming of winter, the permanent rain, and the cholera. The entire chapter, one of the memorable openings in American literature, supplies the novel with a magnificent overture.

The five parts of the book are planned with equal care. Each centers around a single external event, complete in itself yet linked in sequence with the others. In part one Lieutenant Henry is badly wounded at the front. In part two he is removed to a Milan hospital where his shattered knee is operated on successfully. In part three he returns to the front, is caught up in the Italian rout at Caporetto, breaks away from the military police who have been ordered to shoot retreating officers, plunges into the Tagliamento River under a hail of bullets, and manages a breathtaking escape. In part four he rejoins Catherine, and they make their dramatic all-night journey in a rowboat across the lake to Switzerland. In part five Catherine dies in childbirth, and Frederic, as at the start, is once again alone. The death from cholera of seven thousand Italian soldiers at the end of the first chapter has been followed by the two deaths of Catherine and her child at the end of the last. The first disaster is collective and statistical; the second, individual and personal—the two forms in which death appears to us. The novel moves from the general to the particular, from the life-death cycle as an impersonal phenomenon to a heartbreaking sequence of love and separation.

Though death is all around them, the characters never relax their hold on life, their very consciousness of death driving them all the more fervently into the arms of life. Hemingway has been accused of an obsession with death. But such an obsession would mean a subordination of everything to death. His novels indicate the contrary. Though often wounded, even mutilated, though surrounded by premonitions and instances of death, his characters are always turned to life (Harry Street, the narrator of "The Snows of Kilimanjaro," being the conspicuous exception), the presence of death making their consciousness of life all the more acute. The reason for the omnipresence of death in Hemingway's fiction lies here: it provides —and only it can do so—a supreme awareness of life.

As an auxiliary consideration, the man who can face death unflinchingly is the very man who can live life fully.

Hemingway in his own life did not necessarily face death unflinchingly. There is evidence that he did not: he braved it again and again, often gratuitously and recklessly, precisely because he could not face it down. But his art is another matter. Wilson, Manuel Garcia, Macomber eventually, Romero, Jake in his special way, Robert Jordan, Anselmo, and El Sordo in *For Whom the Bell Tolls,* Colonel Cantwell in his own posturing fashion, and in varying degrees the lovers of *A Farewell to Arms* have their several confrontations with death and conquer it in the only way it can be conquered—in the flesh and in the resistant imagination. From Hemingway's point of view this is perhaps the ultimate heroism.

Frederic's responses to the dangers that envelop him are in the same underaccented, underplayed key as Jake's. He does break down occasionally, as Jake does in his night-time sleeplessness. The most severe of Frederic's lapses in self-control comes in the fifth part when, condemned to the role of helpless bystander, he watches Catherine's childbirth agony. But when involved in action himself, he maintains his composure. He is battered by almost the same events as Hemingway was in 1918. He endures without visible buckling the shock of the exploding Austrian mortar shell that shatters his knee, as he does the blood dripping on him from the hemorrhaging soldier in the ambulance. In the hospital he manages to keep from being butchered by incompetent surgeons until a good one comes along who saves his leg. His split-second reaction saves him from the threat of execution in the darkness and rain engulfing the retreating army, and supremely illustrates his physical toughness and mental alertness.

He is also the uncommitted man. He does everything with as little emotion as possible, holding himself in reserve. When asked why he, an American, volunteered for service in the Italian army, he answers jokingly, "Because I was in Italy and I spoke Italian." But it is not altogether a joke. Why indeed did he volunteer? Not because he admired the Italians or enjoyed the military life. Not because it would advance his career—he is studying architecture. Hemingway himself had joined up because the war was glamorous, because he had a taste for adventure and wanted to get away from home. None of these motives seems present in Frederic.

One is forced to conclude that his action is really motiveless, or at any rate without formal motive. It is a private response to a world that makes no great sense. Since the universe is planless, individual conduct might just as well be. Since the cosmos does not appear well thought out or carefully reasoned, whether an individual does one thing or another makes no great difference, and in any case his reasons for pursuing one line of conduct rather than another need not be rationalized, planned, or even definable. Intentions are hardly necessary, or have become out of date. One gives oneself over to drift, to the impulse of the moment. The impulse of the moment may even be a signal from the unconscious self buried deep and hidden from view. Should this prove not so, should the Freudians be wrong, no matter. Nothing has been lost because nothing essential has been altered. The military ambulance corps makes as much sense in the eye of history as the study of architecture. If it turns out that history has no eye, that in the brusque words of the first Henry Ford, "History is bunk," neither good nor harm has been done.

Fifty years after Frederic's enlistment, he might have described his act as going where the action is. With the flow of energy moving toward the front, to remain behind in Rome locked up in the privacy of one's private little pursuit seemed somehow flat. No such reason is supplied by Frederic himself, not because he lacks the brains to dissect his conduct but because he chooses not to, except under extreme pressure. Thinking must be subordinated to living except for emergencies, and then only to keep from going over the deep edge. One of Frederic's rare bouts of reflection comes during Catherine's losing struggle for life when he is in an agony of grief and foreboding, and has nothing to do but sit and wait. Then he has his thoughts about the ants on the burning log.

Most of the time, however, he lives, unreflecting, in the moment. On furlough he does what all the other officers do. When the priest attached to the regiment urges him to visit the Abruzzi, the priest's native region whose clear air, snow-covered mountains, and respectful peasants greatly appeal to Tenente Henry, he half resolves to go there on his next leave; instead he drifts into the same routine of cities, smoke-filled bars, drunken nights when time crumples into a featureless blur, and a deliberate reduction of human relationships to the crudest sexual level. This is his only interest in Catherine when he meets her and for some time thereafter. Because he is self-restrained and unegotistical, he gets along with everyone—banteringly with Rinaldi, the young surgeon who is his closest friend, effectively with the medical orderlies under him, and respectfully with the priest even as the priest is being cruelly and jeeringly baited by the other officers. There is a certain wariness about his manner—always the sign of a man who is unwilling or afraid to give too much of himself. Giving oneself and giving oneself away are firmly equated in his mind.

All this changes when he falls in love with Catherine. The way has been prepared for the change by the priest. The night before Frederic meets Catherine for the first time, he is talking with the priest at the officers' mess. The following cryptic thought passes through his mind: "He had always known what I did not know and what, when I learned it, I was always able to forget. But I did not know that then, although I learned it later." What the "it" is that the priest knows is the meaning of love. Later, at the field hospital where Frederic is convalescing from his wound, the priest comes to visit him, and they have a conversation about love.

> *"When you love you wish to do things for. You wish to sacrifice for. You wish to serve."*
>
> *"I don't love."*
>
> *"You will. I know you will. Then you will be happy."*
>
> *"I'm happy. I've always been happy."*
>
> *"It is another thing. You cannot know about it unless you have it."*

Very soon afterward, in Milan, the priest's predic-

tion comes true. Frederic does fall in love. He does
wish to sacrifice for and serve Catherine. He is carried
out of himself. The protective barrier of wariness and
reserve is broken through, and thus exposed, Frederic
becomes more human and more vulnerable. He becomes as dependent on Catherine as she on him, so
that when she leaves him for as much as two hours,
he feels nervous and depressed, and tries hard not to
think. After his desertion from the army, he finds himself with nothing to do. The usual things are no longer
enough. Fishing, eating and drinking, pleasant conversations with friendly barmen, billiards and champagne
with wise and agreeable old gentlemen like the ninety-
four-year-old Count Greffi, the casual, sensory, pleas-
ure-yielding world, are now insufficient. Only Catherine can fill the vacuum. He is no longer his own man;
he is hers. His carefully nurtured aloofness and
independence have vanished. The world, through
Catherine, has gotten at him. Even after she dies, he
insists on remaining with her. But "it wasn't any good.
It was like saying good-by to a statue. After a while
I went out and left the hospital and walked back to
the hotel in the rain."

These are the last lines of the novel. They wind
up a brilliant rendering of the first-person narrator,
who alone in *A Farewell to Arms* experiences a true
emotional change. If Catherine had gone through an

analogous transformation, the novel would have been the twentieth-century *Anna Karenina*. Hemingway's deepest psychological insights, however, are limited to men. His women fall into two set categories: nihilist and destructive (Lady Brett and Margot Macomber), or sentimental and self-effacing (Catherine, Maria, and Renata). These are limited categories to begin with, and Hemingway does little to expand them. This is especially true of his self-effacing women, who tend to be obscured by the personalities of the men they love.

On the subject of war, which Hemingway studied and pursued most of his life, *A Farewell to Arms* is especially informed. It covers nearly all phases of war, from armament and military strategy to the psychology of individual soldiers and the propaganda of patriotism. *A Farewell to Arms* could almost serve as a manual on trench warfare; *For Whom the Bell Tolls* could do the same for the tactics of guerrilla war. Hemingway, indeed, wrote manuals throughout his career on subjects that absorbed him: there is, for example, his book on bullfighting, *Death in the Afternoon*. Instructions on fishing, boxing, hunting, and soldiering are worked into his narratives. He did not study these activities for "research" purposes or to supply his stories with "authentic" background. He was absorbed in them as an aficionado, which is why he pursued them with such scholarly zeal.

What makes his account of men at war so effective is again its sensory immediacy. Here is the Austrian mortar shell approaching Tenente Henry as he sits in a dugout eating cheese and drinking wine:

> *I heard a cough, then came the chuh-chuh-chuh-chuh—then there was a flash, as when a blast-furnace door is swung open, and a roar that started white and went red and on and on in a rushing wind. I tried to breathe but my breath would not come and I felt myself rush bodily out of myself and out and out and out and all the time bodily in the wind. I went out swiftly, all of myself, and I knew I was dead and that it had all been a mistake to think you just died. Then I floated, and instead of going on I felt myself slide back. I breathed and I was back.*

After recovering from the blast, he becomes aware that he is wounded. The darkness of the dugout is striated by bursts of light from star shells.

> *I sat up straight and as I did so something inside my head moved like the weights on a*

> *doll's eyes and it hit me inside in back of my*
> *eyeballs. My legs felt warm and wet and my*
> *shoes were wet and warm inside. I knew*
> *that I was hit and leaned over and put my*
> *hand on my knee. My knee wasn't there.*
> *My hand went in and my knee was down on*
> *my shin. I wiped my hand on my shirt and*
> *another floating light came very slowly*
> *down and I looked at my leg and was very*
> *afraid. Oh, God, I said, get me out of here.*

The moment is one of horror, yet the description is almost scientifically detached. There is even the remarkable touch of Frederic wiping his bloody hand on his shirt after discovering his knee is not there. The detachment is suddenly broken by his pitiful cry for escape. This combination of the observing eye, which seems to function by itself as an autonomous recording mechanism, and the suffering self, involved in its own subjective pain, is forged by Hemingway as the instrument that enables him to be simultaneously inside and outside an action as it unfolds. It is an instrument that he manages with unfaltering poise.

It is given its severest test in the forty pages covering the retreat from Caporetto, the greatest Italian disaster of the war. Caught up in the retreat, Lieutenant Henry is concerned both with his own safety and the safety of his men and medical vans. Yet while he is maneuvering his way in the rain through muddy roads, blocked highways, and stalled equipment, he has time to note the swarms of refugees fleeing from the advancing Germans. Two frightened young girls, looking like a pair of wild birds, hitch a ride with Frederic's group until the trucks stall in the mud and have to be abandoned. Two sergeants from another unit who joined them decide to bolt instead of helping with the trucks, and Frederic is forced to kill one of them. Italian battle police, in panic, begin to fire at anything that moves; a stray bullet dispatches Aymo, an orderly whom Frederic liked as well as anyone he ever knew.

There is a magnificent sequence of small individual incidents, dramatic in themselves and, together, incarnating the dazed, bedraggled, disorganized spirit of the whole retreat. The affair ends for Frederic with his "separate peace" at the Tagliamento. Again he records what is happening while himself an actor in the drama—a kind of double vision that is the essence of Hemingway's genius for describing physical events.

The comments scattered through the book on the war in general are made during those occasional moments when the characters drop their own immediate problems to consider the huge upheaval of which they are the smallest parts. The comments are usually cynical, sometimes funny, and always intelligent. Old

Count Greffi agrees that the war is stupid, but thinks that Italy will win because she is a younger nation, and younger nations always win wars until they become older nations. An English major at the club in Milan has an equally original view: "He said we were all cooked. The thing was not to recognize it. The last country to realize they were cooked would win the war." In the middle of the war, with no end in sight, Frederic reflects: "Perhaps wars weren't won any more. Maybe they went on forever. Maybe it was another Hundred Years' War." Before he is wounded, Frederic has the euphoric feeling of absolute safety: "I knew I would not be killed. Not in this war. It did not have anything to do with me. It seemed no more dangerous to me myself than war in the movies." And then adds wryly: "Maybe the Austrians would crack. They had always cracked in other wars. What was the matter with this war?"

The war outlasts the lovers. It stands as a permanent part of things, a misfortune that within the framework of the novel will never end. After all the euphoria, the wishful thinking, and the shrewd military analyses are over, the war is still there, as eternal, it would seem, as the mountains and rivers over which it is fought. It starts as a giant intrusion in everyone's life, then settles down to being always there. To get away from it, as Frederic and Catherine finally do, involves a massive and dangerous effort.

The annihilating war does have one purifying effect: it separates false feelings from true. Frederic is nauseated by the old beliefs embodied in such words as sacred, glorious, sacrifice, hallow, and honor. He finds these words obscene. The ideals they invoke, celebrated in patriotic proclamations, are refuted by the slaughter of the war. In the war experience what survives as valid is what the soldier gains through the purging intimacy of physical contact: the names of villages and rivers, the numbers of regiments and roads, anything concrete in space and time. To Hemingway, ideology is anathema. The only truth is what can be tested and verified through the senses.

He expressed his contemporaries' bitter disillusionment with the lofty slogans of the First World War, especially the Wilsonian slogans of making the world safe for democracy and the war to end wars. Behind all this was the nineteenth-century liberalism that the war discredited, the liberalism that believed man to be a rational creature who could be relied upon to create a millennium on earth. The pre-war liberals had accepted as their own Descartes' famous assertion, "I think, therefore I am." Frederic has his reply to it: "I was not made to think. I was made to eat." This elevation of body over mind expresses the ironic mood of a whole generation. The mind, treacherous, intricate, and abstract, must accede to the superior reality of flesh.

The perpetual presence of war in *A Farewell to Arms* also stimulates a considerable amount of religious discussion. It begins with the young Italian priest, a Christlike figure who endures the constant baiting of the anticlerical officers without losing his composure. Frederic is deeply drawn to him, and they have a series of conversations in which Frederic confesses that he is religious only at night. In the daytime he feels nothing. This half-and-half attitude toward God makes him an ideal middle figure between the absolute belief of the priest and the absolute disbelief of Rinaldi. Catherine has no real religious convictions, though she gives Frederic a St. Anthony's medal to protect him. Her only religion, as she says, is being in love with Frederic. Count Greffi, approaching a hundred, is astonished to discover that as he grows older he has become less and less religious. This is a phenomenon for which he cannot account. He must therefore ask his friends to pray for him. He petitions Frederic to pray for him if he, Frederic, ever becomes devout. Frederic promises to pray for him whether he becomes devout or not.

The burning issue linking the war and religion, the

question of how the Catholic Italians and the Catholic Austrians can slaughter each other while invoking the aid of the same God, is touched upon but proves to be a mystery too baffling for comprehension. The novel contents itself with what it can unravel: the actual sentiments of the characters themselves. Theological abstractions and religious mysteries retreat, as always in Hemingway, before the concrete feelings of the individuals involved.

This is reflected in the characteristic style of the novel, with its direct, simple, concrete statements usually connected by *and,* Hemingway's favorite conjunction.

> *The mountain that was beyond the valley and the hillside where the chestnut forest grew was captured and there were victories beyond the plain on the plateau to the south and we crossed the river in August and lived in a house in Gorizia that had a fountain and many thick shady trees in a walled garden and a wistaria vine purple on the side of the house.*

And is primarily a conjunction of time, telling us that the clauses it connects are happening at the same time or one after the other. It calls attention to, indeed concentrates on the present moment, the moment that will never come again. This is exactly what Hemingway intends. His principal aim is immediacy. He therefore tries to free his sentences of every distracting element. He dispenses with cause-and-effect relationships. He uses as few subordinate constructions, dependent clauses, qualifying phrases, and descriptive epithets as possible. In this way he confronts us with a minimum of complicated mental activity, and the action can be released with no distraction. Hemingway's sentences are not "natural"; he strips and prunes them too much. His goal is not naturalness, but an instant flow of energy between the event inside the printed word and the reader.

However much Conrad may have been his moral tutor, in style Hemingway looked elsewhere for guidance, to vernacular writers like Mark Twain and masters of description like the classic nineteenth-century Russian novelist Turgenev. His idiom is at the opposite end of the scale from the baroque of Henry James, Conrad, and Faulkner. *A Farewell to Arms* does not seek to immortalize its lovers and soldiers by analyzing them in depth. It hopes instead to seize them in time, to preserve the freshness of their feelings at the moment of inception and for the brief period thereafter that they retain their purity and intensity. To this end a style based on time linkages, concentrating on the moment at hand, is the logical instrument. The Impressionist painters, whom Hemingway had carefully studied in the Luxembourg Museum, were obsessed with seizing the quality of light before it faded. Hemingway was equally obsessed with catching the sensory moment before *it* faded.

In their last meeting in Milan before he returns to the front, Frederic quotes to Catherine the lines from Andrew Marvell's poem: "But at my back I always hear/ Time's wingèd chariot hurrying near." The lovers are acutely conscious of time passing and wish to make the most of what they have. Marvell reminds them of this urgency. It is the same urgency, before the same remorseless rush of time, that Hemingway seeks to express throughout *A Farewell to Arms*.

4 FOR WHOM THE BELL TOLLS

Between the Armistice of 1918 and Hitler's invasion of Poland in 1939, the supreme emotional event on the international scene was the Spanish civil war. Though fought in a remote corner of Europe, in a country still living under semifeudal conditions, it aroused violent feelings and ferocious partisanship in the outside world. It did so even among those who had never been to Spain and knew nothing about the country.

Politically the war split its partisans straight down the middle. On the side of the government was everyone to the left of center; on the rebel side, led by General Franco, was everyone to the right. The split between them was irreconcilable. The government was supported by the working classes, trade unions, liberals, Socialists, Communists, anarcho-syndicalists, the Basques, and the Catalans. The rebels were backed by the large landowners, the Church, professional army officers, peasants, royalists, and Fascists. It was a conflict that aroused every conceivable political passion, and divided so neatly along ideological lines that few had trouble choosing sides. Fascist Italy and

110

Nazi Germany rushed to help Franco. To the dismay of liberals everywhere, the democracies of France, England, and the United States—the Spanish government's natural friends—folded their arms and declared their neutrality, leaving Soviet Russia, with its own devious motives, the only country willing if not altogether able to support the government.

In the early twenties Hemingway had interviewed Mussolini and had developed a strong dislike for Il Duce. But his interest in politics had never been great and had faded since he had given up newspaper work for writing. It is doubtful that a civil war in Africa, Asia, or South America would have drawn him out of his political indifference. Spain, however, was the one country certain to arouse him. He had been there often, knew and loved its language, landscape, people, and institutions, had been for years deeply involved with bullfighting, and had used Spain as the scene for a number of short stories, *Death in the Afternoon,* and a decisive part of *The Sun Also Rises.* The Spanish civil war moved him as did few other events in his life. In order to get to the heart of the action, Hemingway went to Spain as a foreign correspondent accredited to the government. From this vantage point he was to assemble the impressions, materials, and finally the theme of *For Whom the Bell Tolls.*

His first problem in writing the novel was the question of morality. Were the government forces "good guys" and the rebels "bad"? At first impression it would seem so—just as it would seem so overwhelmingly a few years later in the war against the Nazis. Hemingway, however, did not wish to write a moral tract, another *Pilgrim's Progress* to guide the innocent on the path of righteousness, or a novel in the proletarian style with the virtuous workers winning out against the greedy bosses. As always, his concern was with the romance and tragedy of individual life. Political and social institutions influenced it but, in his aesthetic design, were subordinate elements. The Spanish government may have had political and social institutions superior to those of Franco, but in the distribution of human vices and virtues neither had a monopoly. They were all Spaniards, and while Hemingway found the Spaniards brave, dignified, and hospitable, he also found them treacherous, divisive, incurably factional, and endowed with a passion for killing.

Morally, if not politically, he saw little difference between Loyalists and Fascists. Hemingway tells his story from the viewpoint of a Loyalist guerrilla band, but his Loyalists as men and women are no better or worse than the rebels. By thus separating politics from ethics, Hemingway avoided the danger of weighting his novel in advance. He goes out of his way in other respects to establish the common humanity—and inhumanity—of both sides. In a savage offstage scene Maria, the young heroine of the novel, is raped by the Fascists. In an equally savage chapter, this time onstage, the republicans of Pablo's village massacre the local residents sympathetic to Franco. And Hemingway never lets us forget the powerful position of the Communists in the government war effort. There is the sympathetic and intelligent General Golz, on loan from the Soviet army, who gives Robert Jordan his instructions about blowing up the bridge, a key move to be coordinated with a Loyalist offensive led by Golz. But the effort is largely nullified by the blundering stupidities of the senile André Marty, an actual French Communist whom Hemingway plants unaltered in the Loyalist high command. The Fascist Lieutenant Berrendo, the guerrillas' chief local antagonist, is presented respectfully. As a writer, Hemingway succeeded in liberating himself from the ardent partisanship for the republicans which he felt as a man.

The importation of foreigners tended not only to inflame the outside world's responses to the war but also to blur the moral issues. It was easy to denounce Nazis flying German planes in the Fascist cause, but how was a supporter of democracy to regard the Soviet generals leading government troops on the ground? Mussolini sent a whole Italian division to fight for

Franco, and there were decidedly non-Spanish Moors imported from North Africa to attack the republicans; while an international brigade, assembled from a score of countries, and heavily interlarded with Communists and Communist sympathizers, enlisted in the Loyalist ranks. One of the leading aviators in the tiny government air force was André Malraux, the distinguished and at that time radical novelist, whose *Man's Fate,* an account of the Chinese revolution in the twenties, was an epic of the twentieth century. Robert Jordan, the hero of Hemingway's novel, is an American; his predecessor as saboteur with Pablo's band—slain in the line of duty as Robert Jordan would be in his turn—was a Russian. Hemingway made use of this whole complex mixture of fact and fiction, of history and imagination, to free his work of the rigid moral partisanship that might have, by the very nature of the Spanish civil war, limited his freedom of action as a novelist.

Another problem was language. Everyone in the novel is in Spain, speaking Spanish. How could the Spanish vernacular be conveyed in a book written in English without making it sound either stilted or unconvincing? Hemingway makes no attempt to convert the rhythms of Spanish into English speech patterns: the guerrilla fighters in the Guadarrama Mountains are not awkwardly endowed with an equivalent

American dialect. He tries instead to preserve the Spanish grammar and word order as much as possible, changing it only when it threatens to sound grotesque. The reader is always conscious of being in a foreign country, listening to another tongue that a reasonably skillful translator is making it possible for him to follow. The effect is to make everyone sound more formal, dignified, and elevated than they probably would in real life.

Since the novel deals with critical issues of life and death, the heightened quality of all this, even its very artificiality, is curiously effective. A good deal of the book consists of thoughts passing through Jordan's mind. These, of course, are in English and contrast dramatically with the flow of his language when he is actually speaking. As a teacher of Spanish in a Montana college, as an enthusiast who knows more about Spain than most Spaniards, his Spanish is as authoritative as his English. To have a bilingual expert at the center of the story—a role as important as his being an expert dynamiter—is a great advantage in a novel that oscillates between two languages.

There are minor irritations. A good many Spanish phrases are scattered through the conversation. Afraid that his readers will have no idea what they mean, Hemingway provides instant translations. A Spaniard saying "matador de toros" will at once add "bullfighter." This suggests that the author thinks his readers are morons and makes the characters sound like Berlitz instructors. Another difficulty is the rendering of curse words. Spanish is peculiarly rich in profanity, and everyday speech is replete with it. The unrestrained printing of four-letter words, common today, was far less so in 1940. Joyce and D. H. Lawrence were still regarded as avant-garde writers, and *Lady Chatterley's Lover* was still banned. Instead of resorting to dashes, Hemingway hit upon the word "obscenity" as an all-purpose substitute. "You are an obscenity and the son of an obscenity" and "I obscenity in your mother's milk" are typical examples. The effect of the profane word is conveyed without being actually used.

After the reader gets over the initial surprise, it works well enough. The code word is taken for granted and fades into the background, much as the original profanity does when used often enough. But the convention remains an artificial device, contributing to the sense of artificiality already created by the quasi-literal translation of Spanish into English. This makes the novel more remote from the reader than either *The Sun Also Rises* or *A Farewell to Arms,* which adds something to its quality as an epic but at the loss of intimacy and immediacy. The more impersonal nature of the novel may have persuaded Hemingway to write it in the third person. Jordan is the first of Hemingway's major protagonists not cast as narrator. The stylized effect is further intensified, awkwardly, in the perpetual reference to the hero by his whole name. He is always called Robert Jordan, never Robert or Jordan—an affectation that puffs him up more than is necessary and that again seems a mechanical procedure designed to lift the novel above the ordinary and natural.

Another small irritation is Jordan's pet name for Maria. The two are lovers, under circumstances even more poignant and romantic than Frederic and Catherine's, yet he keeps calling her "rabbit." Every time he does, some of the high seriousness oozes out of their relationship. If Antony were to call Cleopatra "sweetie" or Aeneas address Dido as "doll," the bathos could not be more jarring. Yet their lovemaking in the sleeping-bag, on the ground outside the cave of the guerrillas, is described in terms so lofty as to border on awe, as though this were one of the great emotional experiences in history. More than once Jordan is so transported that he feels the earth moving under him, making the affair an event in geology as well as in love. Within so large a framework Maria's nickname is all the more unfailingly ridiculous.

In general, this love affair is the one serious weakness of *For Whom the Bell Tolls*. The character of

Maria is even less developed than Catherine's, though she is required to carry an even greater emotional responsibility. She and Jordan know each other for only three days. Into those three days everything between them must be crowded. Their love must appear, flower, rise to a record-breaking amatory pitch, reach ecstatic heights, and give Jordan a last experience of supreme earthly joy before his death. Despite the "rabbit" business, he holds up his end of it reasonably well. He has, after all, been at the center of the book from the start. We have been close witnesses of his every thought and act in a multitude of situations, and have come to know him well. He is a revealed figure and therefore sustains the emotion required of him. Maria is unrevealed, undeveloped, and unrealized. She is seen not in her own right but only fitfully through the eyes of Jordan and Pilar, the indomitable woman who holds the band together. Maria does not have, as Catherine does, even those small mannerisms that fill out the edges of a character. She is blank both at the center and at the periphery of her visible self. Yet this embryonic figure is expected to generate, express, and sustain a great passion. The result is disastrous.

Spanish critics of the novel have complained of its ethnic errors. Arturo Barea observed that in real life Pilar, a gypsy, and Pablo, a former horse dealer, would never have been accepted as leaders by a band of Castilian guerrilleros. The differences in background would have been too great. Furthermore the Spaniards would be incapable of organizing a mass slaughter as though it were a fiesta—as in the story of the village massacre told by Pilar. Nor would any Spanish girl go straight to a man's arms as Maria goes to Jordan's, nor be so ignorant of love and even of kissing. These infractions of truth, if they can be called that, are a greater obstacle to Spanish readers than to non-Spanish. They are like the dozens of mistakes in observation Milton commits in his early nature poems "L'Allegro" and "Il Penseroso." He has skylarks perching on window sills, flowers blooming in the wrong season, and the like. This is no doubt disturbing to a botanist, who might even invalidate the poems because of their scientific inaccuracies. To the general reader it makes little difference; the basis of the poems is not primarily factual. Similarly Hemingway's Spanish novel does communicate an overwhelming sense of Spain and its people, and remains undamaged by occasional mistakes in social detail.

In the *Poetics,* Aristotle remarks that the two most important elements in tragedy are character and action, and of the two, action is the more important. In this sense *For Whom the Bell Tolls* is thoroughly

Aristotelian. It has an ample roster of characters, but the action of the novel comes first. What the characters think and what they are is subserved to what they do. This is entirely in keeping with Hemingway's conviction that ideas derive from sensory reactions. He once said to Fitzgerald that the real death of a writer came when he stopped seeing, not when he stopped feeling, for all feeling depended on physical perception.

The principal action is the demolition of a bridge held by the rebels, with Jordan as the dynamiter assigned to the task. Though the bridge is a small one in a remote mountain area, it is of supreme importance, for a Loyalist surprise offensive depends on its destruction. Only a handful of men are involved, but a whole campaign hinges on their efforts. These strategic details supply Hemingway with an ideal dramatic situation, where he can concentrate upon a single small incident on which, however, great events depend.

The sense of microcosm is worked out exquisitely. In the actual war tens of thousands of soldiers were involved on both sides, yet the novel concentrates on no more than a dozen. The war dragged on for three years; the novel lasts three days. Hundreds of aircraft took part in the conflict; only three Fascist planes appear in the book, during the brief raid on El Sordo's hill. Scores of generals, colonels, and other high-rank-ing officers were enrolled in the war; the guerrillas are not divided by rank, and even Jordan, in charge of the operation, has no title; aside from Golz and Marty, the only significant officer to appear is Lieutenant Berrendo, in charge of the enemy patrol opposing Pablo, El Sordo, and their men.

Yet no more care, no more delicate planning, went into Austerlitz and Stalingrad than into the blowing up of this one rickety bridge. The master strategist of the tiny affair is Jordan, and he has to work his way carefully through a maze of obstacles, physical and psychological, to carry out his assignment. His progress through the maze is what the novel is about. Though the objective is a small one, the tactical problems are formidable, reproducing in miniature form much larger and more celebrated military enterprises. The odds are against success. Jordan does not have enough men, and even some of them are unreliable. He comes as a stranger and a foreigner, and yet must win loyalty almost at once. The Fascists are far better armed and can call up heavy reinforcements quickly. The weather must be favorable. The element of surprise must work. Indeed, a dozen variables must work, or the project is doomed.

The men Jordan must count on present their own problems. Pablo, the leader, shrewd, vain, highly intelligent, has lost his nerve and is against attacking the bridge. He sees all the dangers and is sure the plan will fail. He poisons the morale of the others, who hate and despise him, and hope that Jordan will shoot him as a menace to the operation. In a tense confrontation Jordan almost does, but Pablo's willingness to swallow insults and the American's reluctance to kill unless unavoidable save the guerrilla leader. Afterward Jordan regrets his hesitation and feels he has made a mistake. Also the band has fallen into a defensive mood, preferring to hole up in the safety of their cave rather than expose themselves to the dangers of fighting in the open. Jordan must somehow reverse their frame of mind and persuade them into aggressive action. Aside from their responses as a group, each man has his own individual sensitivities, and Jordan must thread his way through a minefield of subtle emotion which at every moment threatens to explode in his face.

By no means the least of Jordan's problems are those arising from himself. He is plagued with doubts about everything. He has doubts about the war. He volunteered because of his love for Spain and his devotion to democracy, but the Communists have assumed more and more control over the government war effort. Jordan is not a Communist; he actively distrusts Communism. But he is anti-Fascist and on that basis, despite growing reservations, continues to fight.

He is of the same divided mind about the Spaniards—
a wonderful people in many ways but terrible in others.

His political misgivings are matched by his personal ones. Jordan's father had committed suicide, an
act that infected his son with a persisting sense of
shame. Jordan associates himself with his grandfather,
a Union hero in the American Civil War who had
fought against slavery. But his father's ultimate weakness is always in his mind. Will he, too, be a coward
in a moment of crisis? He wants to prove worthy of
his grandfather. He wants to behave bravely and erase
the memory of his father's deed. Yet here, too, he is
afflicted with doubt.

He also has premonitions of his own death, which
he tries hard to put aside. But they return periodically
to eat away at his reserves of nervous energy, especially as the hour for the attack on the bridge draws
near. Shortly after he meets Pilar, who is a fortune-
teller, she insists on reading his palm. What she sees
in his hand—his coming death, obviously—fills her
with such foreboding that she refuses to tell him what
is there and passes it off lightly. He knows, and of
course we know, what she has seen. This brief incident, granting that its message is crudely arranged,
nevertheless dramatizes the terrible danger that hangs
over him and aggravates his fear.

A final complication is his love for Maria, which

naturally increases his desire to live and diminishes his willingness to risk death. Unlike Romeo and Frederic Henry, Jordan falls in love at first sight. The moment he sets eyes on Maria he feels a "thickness in his throat." Tenderness and the heat of sexual appetite flood over him simultaneously, and over her as well. Their senses are ignited; their feelings aroused; their relationship consummated almost at once. The wholeness, the releasing power of love, which most human beings struggle to attain, comes to them immediately and effortlessly. Hemingway grants it to them not because they deserve it more than others do, not because they are special or remarkable persons, but because it suits the purposes of his novel. It will lend a final poignancy to the attack on the bridge.

The attack has been scheduled for the daytime, making it peculiarly dangerous. The day before the assault Jordan discovers that the Fascists have gotten wind of the Loyalist offensive, have brought up heavy reinforcements, and are fully prepared. He sends a messenger to warn Golz. But it is too late. The offensive begins, though it is doomed to fail. And the dynamiting of the bridge will serve no useful purpose after all.

All the conceivable risks, dangers, and calamities of a great campaign are telescoped into this one minuscule operation. Hemingway is a master of the small panorama. He is expert at describing one man, one incident, one moment, one sensation. Into it, as in a true microcosm, he re-creates the characteristics and the significance of the larger whole. The great enterprises of love, war, friendship, intrigue, and politics are to be found in Jordan's brief encounter with Pablo's band, as small and scruffy a guerrilla group as ever holed up in jungle or mountainside. The quotation from John Donne, that Hemingway uses as his epigraph, eloquently asserts the interconnection and interdependence of all things: "No man is an *Iland,* intire of it selfe; every man is a peece of the *Continent,* a part of the *maine* . . . . any mans *death* diminishes *me,* because I am involved in *Mankinde;* And therefore never send to know for whom the *bell* tolls; It tolls for *thee.*" What happens to Jordan is part of a universal process embracing the rest of the world.

Paradoxically Hemingway pursues his theme of interdependence by examining his characters in a state of isolation. This is a matter of art, not philosophy. His art suggests the collective through the singular, implies the genre through the individual, alludes to the many outside the field of immediate vision by a blazing concentration on the one object before our eye.

His characters' ties with society and the mass of humanity may be indirect and implied. Their ties with nature are immediate. On both the first and last pages of the novel Jordan is lying on the pine-needled floor of the forest. Below him are the mill, the stream, and the bridge with which he is concerned. Above, the pine forest stretches upward to the mountaintop, and beyond that is the sky fleeced with clouds. In the opening scene, accompanied by Anselmo, he is looking at the valley below through a spyglass. In the closing scene, with the bridge successfully destroyed, Jordan is gazing at the path below through the sights of his rifle. He is completely alone. The guerrillas, and Maria with them, are retreating into the back country ahead of the advancing Fascist soldiers. Jordan, his leg broken when his horse slipped and fell upon it, is protecting their retreat at the expense of his own life. Lieutenant Berrendo appears. Just before firing at him, Jordan feels "his heart beating against the pine-needle floor of the forest," and with this sentence the book comes to an end.

Close attention is paid throughout to weather changes, mutations of light, wind currents, the passage of birds, and every detail of the terrain. The earth and its movements extract from Jordan his most alert reactions. These movements are literally a matter of life and death. If the snow comes at the wrong time, if the rays of the sun are too slanting, if the current under the bridge is too swift, the whole enterprise is threatened with collapse. Nature is fiercely present throughout, but its presence is not merely a matter of aesthetics. It is not there because it is beautiful or because it supplies a spectacular background to the story. It is a decisive element in the action. Hemingway dramatizes nature; he does not merely describe it. The Spanish landscape, the Spanish earth are central to the novel and not just its panoramic scene.

The plot revolves around two separate military incidents: the entrapment and killing of El Sordo and his men, and the attack on the bridge. In each, Hemingway pursues his double aim. He is interested in the details of battle for their own sake—in another incarnation he must certainly have been a staff officer in a war college. He is also concerned with plot as an instrument by which character can be established. His ability to project men in action while at the same time keeping them distinct from it is one of the creative secrets of *For Whom the Bell Tolls*. El Sordo's character—coarse, primitive, fearless, calculating—emerges with ferocious clarity during his last stand on the hilltop, while he is being attacked from below by a superior force of rebel troops and from above by unopposed rebel planes. Pablo's men and Pablo himself, put under ultimate pressure during the fight at the bridge, are revealed in their essential qualities: Francisco's stolid, taciturn dignity, Anselmo's spiritual decorum, the core of strength beneath the flightiness of Rafael the gipsy, the blunt honesty of Agustín, and Pablo's absolute shamelessness when it comes to saving his own skin. He swallows insults and blows when his life is at stake, and even accepts the humiliation of being replaced by Pilar as leader of the guerrillas. Since there are not enough horses to allow everyone to escape, Pablo shoots the men who have just fought by his side.

Only Maria remains on the sidelines. Her marginal role is emphasized during the attack on the bridge. Everyone is involved and in mortal peril except her. She is given the task of guarding the horses, well out of danger. Even Pilar, the only other woman on the scene, takes a rifle and fights with one of the assault squads. It is this that finally validates Pilar's earlier stream of talk. Through most of the novel she seizes every chance to discourse, with remarkable vigor and at great length, on the subjects that absorb her: Pablo, death, her former life as the mistress of the bullfighter Finito before she took up with Pablo. She is the chronicler and historian of the novel's events: it is she who narrates in flashback the terrible story of the Fascist villagers slaughtered by their Loyalist neighbors. She reminisces over her own rich, gaudy past. She philosophizes on such matters as the smell of fear and the smell of death. She reads the wavering and unreliable Pablo with corrosive finality.

But until the skirmish at the bridge, it has been just talk. She has not been subjected to the stress of action required to sustain the words. Pilar has been a powerful voice in the novel and a powerful presence, but before her character can be fully realized Hemingway must take her out of the showcase of her own rhetoric and throw her into the combat alongside the men. Her actions, like her speech, are performed with impressive *brio,* and there remains a touch of showy self-consciousness about her presentation, as though the author could not help saying, "Isn't she a great personality!"

Between them she and Jordan supply the book with its polarities. Pilar is female, superstitious, middle-aged. Jordan is male, rational, youthful. She is entirely a creature of instinct and sensation, while he can act freely only on the basis of conviction and principle. As they embody the male and female categories, it is natural that Pilar should be in love with him. "I care for thee very much, *Inglés,*" she says toward the close. He makes her meaning perfectly plain when he replies, "I don't want that now." Both the differences in age and her relationship with Pablo make it impossible for them to become lovers. She does the next best thing. She gives him Maria, a young substitute for herself.

Hemingway's art is compressive. He reduces the world to the small, private, self-enclosed circle of his characters. In his Spanish epic he concentrates on the tiny area of the guerrilla band, caught up in its small private tensions and in the tiny military operation of the bridge. But it exists as part of a larger circle, the country as a whole. The guerrillas are part of the whole republican army. Blowing up the bridge is integral to a large government offensive. The cave in the Guadarramas opens upon the hotels and gathering places like Gaylord's in the great capital of Madrid, which Jordan visits occasionally and where he renews his perspective on the Spanish upheaval in its entirety. Pilar's flashbacks recall Spain before the war, making the present moment part of the larger current of time. The novel flows back and forth in both space and time, but always centering on the few guerrillas engaged in their small three-day action.

The earlier novels, limited to the private sphere, were narrated in the first person, a device deliberately designed to focus on a single consciousness. Their style was the one made famous by Hemingway: hard-boiled, tight-lipped, laconic, epigrammatic—exactly the qualities needed to preserve the isolation of the individual. But excessive introspection was also avoided:

the style stressed dialogue rather than intellectual analysis. As the frame of reference widens in *For Whom the Bell Tolls*—the very title emphasizes human interdependence and solidarity—the style changes as well. The first-person narrator is replaced by the third-person. This enables Hemingway to break out of the confines of the single mind, Jake's or Frederic Henry's, and move freely in any direction. Most of the story is told through Jordan's eyes, but there is time for leisurely penetration into the thoughts of Anselmo, Pablo, Pilar, and the rest. The style stretches. There is a noticeably greater ease and freedom of movement. The barriers between action and feeling, society and self, the outer and inner dimensions, are dissolved. No man is an island unto himself, and Hemingway's rhetoric, now grown expansive, joins the isolated human fragments to the whole.

In *A Farewell to Arms* Lieutenant Henry jeers at slogans like honor and patriotism. Jordan, by contrast, is able to give himself over to the idea, equally abstract, of brotherhood. He is embarrassed by the abused word "crusade," yet he feels himself in Spain to be part of a crusade on behalf of "all of the oppressed of the world." The concept of a binding unity among all things comes to him with great force in his last moments of existence. As he lies on the pine-needle floor of the forest, his leg broken, he is suddenly in contact with everything at once: the enemy about to appear below him, Maria whom he has persuaded not to stay behind with him by assuring her that he is part of her forever, his comrades whose retreat to safety he is shielding with his own life, and the natural world surrounding him: "He took a good long look at everything. Then he looked at the sky. . . . He touched the palm of his hand against the pine needles where he lay and he touched the bark of the pine trunk that he lay behind." Sky, earth, men, fuse into a single unified pattern with Jordan the focal point. For the first time Hemingway can say of him, "He was completely integrated now." The state of complete integration is what the novel has been moving toward, and succeeds in achieving in a single consummated instant before Jordan's death.

Preludes to this had appeared earlier in the book. Among these, one of the most notable and beautifully formulated is chapter fifteen. Here, as dusk falls, old Anselmo is crouched behind a tree watching a sawmill held by the rebels. He has been counting the number of enemy cars passing up and down the road. Though it is early June, a freak snowstorm has started. Anselmo is cold; he doubts that a continued watch is really necessary and wonders whether to abandon his post and go back to the cave. He resolves instead to stay where he is. Jordan's orders had been for him to remain until relieved, and this he will do even if it makes no sense to endanger his well-being by staying out in the freezing dark. He can see the Fascist soldiers through the lighted window of the sawmill. They are poor men as we are, he thinks, and should not be fighting against us. He dislikes the idea of having to kill them the next day. Anselmo dislikes the idea of killing altogether, believes it is a great sin, and thinks that after the war everyone will have to do penance for all the killing. Meanwhile he envies his enemies in their warm shelter while he is shivering outside in the icy wind.

The focus shifts briefly to the soldiers inside. They are glad to be where they are, in a remote outpost far away from the serious fighting. Still, all the staff cars passing that day have made them nervous. Nothing really to worry about, they assure themselves, what with their side's superior air power. The next day, the reader suspects, they will all be dead, a knowledge mercifully and ironically concealed from them.

Back again to Anselmo, still watching in the darkness, still kept there against his better judgment by a stubborn faithfulness to orders. The horror of killing is again in his thoughts. It is bad for everyone. There are those who come to like it, and thus are corrupted. Jordan kills but, Anselmo thinks with relief, he does not like it. In Spain, alas, killing is done too quickly, too easily; then there is much repentance later when it is too late.

At this point Jordan and Francisco come to relieve him, and the three return to the cave. The journey back is presented through Jordan's thoughts. It was a crime to leave Anselmo there so long, but he is tremendously encouraged by the old man's faithfulness. Jordan puts his arm around Anselmo and says, "You don't know what it means to find somebody in this country in the same place they were left." Filled with a sudden, rare sense of happiness, he looks at the taciturn Francisco and wonders if he would stand firm, too. Jordan thinks he just might. And on this note of confidence the three plod up the hill in the snow.

The chapter is strategically placed, at almost the halfway mark of the book. Its tone is quiet, almost serene. Contemplation rather than action is its motif. It is a breathing space, with both sides pausing before the next day's violent and final collision. In this momentary relaxation men are seen in their wholeness. Anselmo thinks of the killing he must do in terms of repentance. He feels friendly toward the enemy soldiers, whom he sees as men much like himself. Jordan is buoyed by Anselmo's fidelity, and extends his exhilaration to cover Francisco. The war is still on, but there are intimations of peace. Darkness is descending, but the light from the sawmill counters it. Everyone is seen in his humanity, thrust unwillingly into the war, yet seeking dissociation from it. For once nature appears in her hostile aspects—darkness descending, snow falling, wind whipping—and man in his steadiness: the chapter is a hymn to Anselmo standing firm. Against the destructive forces of nature, of the war, men hold fast. The theme of the chapter is human wholeness, which is also the theme of the novel's title and the novel itself. A dozen other moments in the narrative prepare the way for the ultimate emotion, Jordan's feeling of integrality at the very end.

For Whom the Bell Tolls is a massive testament to affirmative action. Jordan is in Spain of his own free will, out of love and admiration for the Spaniards, unlike Frederic Henry who is in Italy for no compelling reason. Jordan risks and finally gives his life for the Loyalist cause even after losing his political attachment to it, again unlike Frederic who drifts into the Italian army and leaves it as soon as something else comes up. Jake and Frederic, among Hemingway's earlier heroes, use their resources mainly to survive as men. Jordan's universe is no less discouraging than in *The Sun Also Rises,* but it is life itself in its fullness that he manages to celebrate. The great experiences are open to him, and he reaches them all. He travels, loves, makes friends, leads his comrades in a crucial enterprise, and willingly sacrifices his most precious possession for them. Personal feeling rather than ideological conviction has come to arouse his profoundest loyalty.

Hemingway always preferred the small sensory precisions of Turgenev to the cinemascope canvases of Tolstoy. But *For Whom the Bell Tolls* is his Tolstoyan novel, dealing with nothing less than the destiny of a nation. That destiny is worked out in terms of a small group, and finally of a single man, but sight of the whole is never lost. The emotional opportunities open to the hero are rich, numerous, and complex enough to match the scale on which the novel is conceived. It may not be as perfectly written as *The Sun Also Rises* or as perfectly counterpointed as *A Farewell to Arms*. But it achieves its own peculiar and impressive grandeur.

5 THE MINOR NOVELS

Hemingway wrote three lesser novels. They are not to be ranked with his major works of fiction, though one of them, *To Have and Have Not,* has a number of superb passages. All of them, however, reveal the mind and intentions of the author as vividly as the more successful works. The three were written at roughly twelve-year intervals, appearing in 1926, 1937, and 1950, and seem almost like light exercises among the greater efforts.

The first, *The Torrents of Spring,* was Hemingway's declaration of independence from Sherwood Anderson and Gertrude Stein. Like all parodies it is absolutely dependent on what it is parodying. Unless the reader is familiar with Anderson's novel *Dark Laughter,* the immediate target of Hemingway's satire, or with Miss Stein's hypnotic repetitiousness, *The Torrents of Spring* makes little sense. Taken by itself, it is a baffling tone poem in prose, sounding like the effusion of a talented undergraduate disguising himself as a stammering idiot, but with genuinely funny moments. Given no clues, the reader would have a hard time figuring out what it all means. With Anderson and Stein firmly in mind, however, Hemingway's novel comes into focus. It is a clever mimicry of Anderson's sentimentalized staccato sentences, his attempt to get down to "basics" in feeling and action, his glorification of primitivism, and of Miss Stein's habit of affecting profundity by saying the same thing over and over again in an incantatory tone.

The book is hardly what one enthusiastic critic called "a hilarious and disorderly masterpiece of humor." It goes on too long, as Anderson himself accurately observed when he got over his bewildered astonishment and pain on reading it. But it is an early proof of Hemingway's highly developed ear for speech, sentence rhythm, and even that more subtle process, the movement of ideas—in this case, the ideas of others. It also embodies the paradox of satire: the more it attacks the object it wishes to destroy, the more it immortalizes that object. As long as Hemingway's works are read, Sherwood Anderson will be remembered.

When spring comes to northern Michigan at the start of the novel, the sap rises freely in everyone, intellectual and proletarian alike. Scripps O'Neill, the Harvard intellectual, gets close to nature by picking up a stray bird and carrying it with him wherever he goes. An elderly waitress in the local eatery seems to be uttering essential truths with simple purity; he marries her. A little later a younger waitress supplants the first; her speech seems to Scripps even purer and more richly laced with literary allusions. His relations with these women consists of holding hands, uttering solemn mood statements while gazing vaguely into the distance, and waiting for a mystic fusion. Meanwhile, in the pump factory at the other end of town, Yogi Johnson, the proletarian, also has his vernal dreams. Going to Paris and living around the corner from Gertrude Stein is one of them: "Ah, Paris. . . . Paris in the morning. Paris in the evening. Paris at night. Paris in the morning again. Paris at noon, perhaps. Why not?" His thoughts rattle on in this mindless chant, cleverly reproducing and simultaneously mocking Miss Stein's own vulnerable rhythmics.

Indians abound in *The Torrents of Spring.* They are Anderson primitives, presumably with a deep instinctive wisdom that white men lack. Negroes had been endowed with this superior fount of wisdom in Anderson's novel *Dark Laughter,* and their rich, uninhibited laughter has its equivalent here in the sound of distant redskin war whoops that end several of the chapters. Yogi Johnson is last seen going off into the woods with a naked squaw, shedding his clothes one by one along the railroad track (i.e., shedding his civilized coverings in order to peel down to his natural self). Following him at a discreet distance are two woods Indians, retrieving the garments he is throwing

away. One of them picks up an initialed shirt and remarks, "White chief snappy dresser." These two Indians have not been briefed on *Dark Laughter,* nor
have they heard how much better and more honest it
is to live in the woods than in town.

The satirical drollery reaches its climax in chapter
twelve. The local club is modeled on a white country
club, except that the members are Indians who speak
in polished British accents. They are very exclusive,
and direct their exclusion at white men and at Indians
socially inferior to themselves. When Yogi enters one
evening, accompanied by a pair of nonstatus Indians,
all three are thrown out, despite the fact that one of
the Indians, equipped with artificial arms and legs to
replace the ones he lost in the war, is a great billiards
player, and no indoor game is more fashionably aristocratic than billiards. Still, out they go, their social
and racial defects too serious to be overlooked. This
small incident again illustrates the arrangement on
which the whole novel is based: the exchange of racial
roles in which the whites act as the Indians are supposed to and the Indians behave as the white men do
in fact. The collision of hypothetical Indians played
by whites and real whites played by stage Indians supplies *The Torrents of Spring* with its comic formula.

It is the most "literary" book Hemingway ever
wrote, made up of bits and pieces thrown together

from other writers. The style is imitation Anderson and Stein. Some of the sentiments, especially the parodied search for deep-down real feelings, are borrowed from D. H. Lawrence, one of Anderson's masters. Turgenev supplies the title; and the subtitle, "A Romantic Novel in Honor of the Passing of a Great Race," is in the best tradition of the nineteenth-century popular romance. There is an epigraph from Henry Fielding, the famous eighteenth-century English novelist, and Hemingway borrows Fielding's practice of interrupting the story to speak in his own person. As himself, Hemingway makes comments as he goes along on the novel he is writing and even introduces his own friends and fellow writers, Dos Passos and Fitzgerald, who make brief appearances in the book. The device from Fielding reminds us that Fielding had begun his career as a novelist with two books, *Shamela* and *Joseph Andrews,* both poking fun at Samuel Richardson's *Pamela,* a best seller of the day. Richardson's attachment to virtue and the techniques of defending it had grown as sentimental as Anderson's attachment to self-discovery and the techniques of promoting it. *The Torrents of Spring* is Hemingway's farewell to his apprenticeship, a grab bag of the writers he had read, studied, been influenced by, was still associating with, and was now in the process of freeing himself from. He wrote it in a single quick burst after finishing the

first draft of *The Sun Also Rises,* "to cool out," as
he said. When he had "cooled out," he returned to
rewriting and completing the great novel in which for
the first time he was entirely on his own.

It is a commonplace of psychology that the external
objects we attack are reflections of something in our-
selves. The standard Freudian interpretation of why
Hamlet hesitates to kill his uncle is that in his own
mind he has committed the very crimes his uncle has
committed in actuality. If there is any truth in this,
then in attacking Anderson, Hemingway may be pro-
jecting an anxiety of his own. It is the fear that he,
too, will drown in the swamp of feeling, that in the
pursuit of feeling his ability to distinguish between
true and false feeling, between sentiment and sentimentality, will grow blurred. The cure for this was to
keep emotion under tight control, to concentrate instead on the external situation, to subordinate sentiment to sense impression, to cultivate a laconic,
underaccented tone that would serve as a dike against
the overflow of passion.

In a word, he would create the Hemingway style, in
which action comes first and emotion, if it appears at
all, appears indirectly, its release triggered by the un-
folding of the external moment. One may look upon
The Torrents of Spring not simply as Hemingway's
act of separation from Anderson, but as evidence of

a concealed and dangerous tendency within himself that must be ruthlessly held in check.

To Have and Have Not is Hemingway's depression novel. Its title, ending with "have not," is an obvious reference to the dispossessed. It was written in the mid-thirties, during the author's ten-year stay in Key West, Florida. In the novel, Key West is filled with men on bread lines and families on relief. Harry Morgan, the central figure, is worried about what would become of his wife and two daughters if anything should happen to him; keeping them off relief is one of his major concerns.

Aside from these immediate details, there is a larger aspect of the depression at work in the book, perhaps its controlling aspect. The depression broke up the old laissez-faire procedures of American capitalism, and paved the way for massive Federal intervention, giant trade unions, and the welfare state. It toppled the businessman as the reigning god in the American pantheon and substituted the idea of collective action for the early pioneer idea of individual free enterprise. But at the height of the depression there was a period when the old order was cracking up while the new one was not yet in sight. *To Have and Have Not* appeared at precisely this period, and it is this pattern of disintegration that dominates the book.

The novel emphasizes the absolute separation of rich and poor. Both are present in the story; neither has any contact whatever with the other. When Morgan, dying, is brought in from the sea, he passes the yachts of the rich moored in the harbor. They are totally oblivious to him. Morgan's boat passes theirs at a slow funeral pace, without recognition or acknowledgment of any kind. This scene symbolizes the gulf that exists between the classes, which the depression did much to intensify. Nor is there any significant communication within each class. The wealthy yachtsmen are locked up each in his neurotic isolation. The friction of dislike marks their relations with one another. As for Morgan, a free-lance working "stiff," he is more of a loner than anyone in Hemingway. His one affectional tie is with his wife and children, who seldom appear. His one friend is a hopeless drunk, who sponges off him shamelessly. For the most part, however, he lives in a dog-eat-dog atmosphere of suspicion, hostility, and violence, made more ferocious by the desperate scramble for whatever work was still available during the great economic collapse.

The very structure of the novel contains the idea of disintegration. There are two separate stories, largely unrelated to each other. One deals with Morgan's adventures as a whiskey smuggler between Cuba and Florida, with occasional forays at smuggling Cuban revolutionaries from the mainland and illegal Chinese immigrants to the mainland. The other involves a Hollywood writer named Richard Gordon, who has lost his ability to write and is in the process of losing his wife as well. If Morgan is defeated physically, Gordon is a symbol of emotional and intellectual failure. But their contact is as tangential as the contact between the rich and poor, the haves and have-nots. Morgan and Gordon never meet at all, and the sections about each figure appear without any sign of connection. This separation is the point of the book, the rifts in its structure underlining the vision of a painfully divided society. *To Have and Have Not* has often been criticized because of its fragmentation and disconnectedness. But it is this fragmentation which reflects its theme.

The scenes of violent discord in the novel also suggest the times. The sudden, brutal, quite motiveless brawl of the veterans that wrecks a Florida café is as typical an event as Harry losing an arm in a gun duel with Federal agents at sea while he is illegally running rum from Cuba. People quarrel loudly throughout the book. The bitter arguments between Gordon and his wife all but drown out the troubled tenderness prevailing between the Morgans.

The concept of a collapsing world is present in all of Hemingway's novels. Here for the first time the characters collapse with it. With Jake and his friends, the disaster of the First World War is over before their story begins, and in its aftermath they manage, in their erratic fashion, to keep going. Frederic and Catherine are able to get away from the war and live out their private drama by themselves; this is the meaning of Frederic's separate peace. Jordan is inside a society being torn apart by civil conflict, yet he succeeds in holding his small part of it together and maintaining himself intact. Morgan struggles with equal tenacity to keep afloat but fails, and his failure darkens a novel which in its general outlook is Hemingway's bleakest and most destructive.

Morgan is an immediate victim of the depression. He uses his boat for two purposes: to haul legitimate cargo and to take sportsmen fishing. With the coming of hard times, the legitimate cargo dries up, and he is forced into illegal substitutes: liquor, Chinese coolies, and gunmen fomenting Caribbean revolutions. His chartered fishing trips for wealthy sportsmen suffer similarly. The depression has virtually eliminated them, as the opening scene demonstrates with drastic finality. Morgan's boat is chartered by a Mr. Johnson. They go fishing day after day while Mr. Johnson runs up a large bill. After the fishing is over, he gives Morgan a check that turns out to be bad; by the time

Morgan discovers this, Johnson has fled Cuba, leaving Morgan not only without a profit but in debt for the equipment and gasoline bought for the trip.

This swindle is the root of the subsequent disasters. Morgan is forced, against his better judgment, to smuggle Chinese into the United States; after that, in growingly reckless attempts to earn a living, he engages in an inevitably losing war with the law. He loses an arm in one skirmish; later his boat is confiscated by the Federal authorities. In the end he is driven to the last frantic venture with the Cubans, who rob a bank in Key West to finance a revolution in Havana. On the trip over they murder Harry, though he succeeds, in a final exhibition of courage and power, in liquidating them as well.

The bad times bring Morgan down. Were it not for the general economic breakdown, he would have continued operating his boat, legally and uneventfully, as he had done before. He cannot adjust to the disaster. It is too large and complex for his individual energies. Morgan himself finally realizes this. With his last breath he says, "One man alone ain't got. . . . No matter how a man alone he ain't got no bloody chance." Whatever was wrong with society, men acting alone could not put it right. The thirties were to demonstrate that the cure depended on collective action. But all that came later, too late for Morgan who, being what he was, could not have adjusted to it even had he lived.

For he is the supreme loner, and as such, a throwback to pioneer times. The man who relied entirely on himself, who looked upon the government as an enemy, who went forth to conquer the wilderness, push back the frontier, and settle the land, was Morgan's prototype. Mass production made him obsolete, and its breakdown in 1929 revealed him as a person with no place to go. In the old days he could walk away from social and economic problems by moving westward into free land, to be taken through his own unaided efforts. He had free will because he had free land. One depended on the other. With the country settled and free land gone, he was displaced and rendered helpless. Huck Finn could always light out for the Territory when things got too uncomfortable at home. In Harry Morgan's time there was no territory to light out for. He managed to escape from the settled, overcrowded earth to water, but even the free expanse of water was no longer free. Every country in the Caribbean had coast-guard cutters, chopping up the sea into controllable segments, boxing in those who sought to maneuver on their own. When the government impounded his boat, Morgan was disarmed and rendered as impotent as a medieval knight who had lost his sword or a cowboy his horse.

Morgan was named after the famous pirate of the eighteenth century who operated in the Caribbean, a clue to his own freebooting character. He is the single, solitary, unaccompanied man. He has no friends, partners, or associates. Eddy, the drunk, the one person who does stay near him, is only in his way, and Morgan is always trying to get rid of him. At one point he seriously contemplates killing Eddy, as he does indeed ruthlessly and deliberately kill Mr. Sing. He does so to save a dozen other Chinese, yet he kills without a qualm. But he is not without heart. He has a contemptuous affection for Eddy. He genuinely loves his wife, though his relationship with her is essentially that of the primitive hunter going off alone for long periods to forage for his family.

Morgan is tall, well built, and all "man," as his wife recalls in lamentation after his death. But he is utterly mindless. He is great with guns and boats, but not a thought unconnected with immediate physical survival ever occurs to him. He has no curiosity, no power to contemplate anything not immediately visible, and in a sense no personality. It is not so much that he is stupid—he obviously is not—as that he is unrealized. His intelligence, his capacity for general

ideas, his emotional sensibilities, are simply undeveloped. Hemingway whittles him down to a pure
pragmatic instrument, all body and driving will but
little feeling and no brain, a superb half man. This is
the novel's gravest weakness. Its central figure reduces
it to the most elementary sensory level, and the emotion that is supposed to be released by the sensory
moment is hardly there. Morgan is too blank for that.
The life of the spirit that extends beyond the purely
physical is absent in him. And in this respect, too, he
is unique among Hemingway's heroes, all of whom are
highly intelligent, responsive, and observant men.

Taken by itself, the action in *To Have and Have
Not* may be self-enclosed and fail to arouse a large
enough range of feeling, but it is mastered on its own
terms as brilliantly as anywhere in Hemingway. The
strength of the novel lies here. The fishing and shooting, the talk, the drinking, the lovemaking, the fist-
fights are described with extraordinary concreteness.
The immediate, tangible world lights up at once. The
novel may lack insight and depth, but it is long on
physical impressions. Morgan lives entirely in the
sensory flow; everything he touches and sees leaps
straight to the equivalent sense of the reader, his very
lack of personality facilitating the process. The distance between us and the actual events all but dis-
appears.

Though limited in scope and bounded on all sides by purely physical dimensions, this is nonetheless an uncanny achievement. Hemingway's art is seen at its narrowest, but what it lacks in breadth it makes up for in descriptive power. The projection of the physical world is so complete that the absence of mind is almost made up for. Almost, though not quite. *To Have and Have Not* is like Morgan himself. It is, finally, one-armed.

Among his other impacts, Hemingway has exerted a powerful influence on the hard-boiled detective story. Dashiell Hammett, an early master of the genre, took his cue mainly from the stories of *In Our Time* and *Men Without Women*. Raymond Chandler and Ross Macdonald derive straight from *To Have and Have Not*. Their celebrated private eyes—Sam Spade, Philip Marlowe, and Lew Archer—are variants of Harry Morgan. They, too, are physically tough, cynical about the human prospect, and at home with cruelty and violence. They, too, conceal a core of tenderness and sentiment beneath a hard exterior.

The world they inhabit is a duplicate of Morgan's, the world of every man for himself with survival the universal objective. Their locale is the big-city jungle where even the hunted are themselves hunters, whose dominant pattern is the labyrinth from which few emerge intact. Amid the constant pursuits, the perpetual exchange of blows, the universal confusion and din, these men manage to snatch an occasional moment of warmth or love, a fleeting interlude of sincere human expression—significant grace notes in the general discord. Their thoughts, their prose, are pared down to the necessities of survival. It is a style free of verbiage (though Chandler has a penchant for graceful, even brilliant metaphors), and adapted to the quick flow of physical action. Like those who speak it and think it, it is prose that travels light.

These are the same qualities visible in Hemingway's stories and lesser novels. In the great novels they blend with other tones and colorations, and are less nakedly evident. But in *To Have and Have Not,* where these tones and colorations are notably absent, they stand out with overwhelming starkness. In one of Raymond Chandler's thrillers, *Farewell, My Lovely,* the following exchange takes place:

> *"Who is this Hemingway person?"*
> *"A guy [says Marlowe] that keeps say-*
> *ing the same thing over and over until you*
> *begin to believe it must be good."*

No left-handed compliment ever registered an influence more succinctly.

Across the River and Into the Trees, the last of Hemingway's minor novels, is a thoroughly irritating book. It is the most intimately personal of his works, the one Hemingway felt closest to, where almost no difference exists between author and hero. They are the same age, fifty. Like Hemingway, Colonel Cantwell loves Venice, has a body full of wounds and scars symbolized in the story by his failing heart, is an enthusiastic duck hunter, an aficionado of fist fighting, war, and the problems of military combat, a lover of beautiful women, and a dogmatic connoisseur of food, drink, and manners. The novel is largely a monologue running through the Colonel's head during the last weekend of his life, a monologue devoted to unqualified self-praise.

The novel is an aggressive exercise in narcissism. Much of it displays Cantwell looking in a mirror, or carefully examining his conduct and characteristics past and present and finding them good. He is proud of his wounds and even loves his battered face. When he is not talking or thinking to himself about his splendid qualities, he is engaged in a dialogue with a nineteen-year-old Italian countess named Renata, with whom he is having a love affair. The two spend much of their time proclaiming, even less convincingly than Frederic and Catherine, what wonderful people they are. Cantwell praises her beauty, charm, and aristocratic breeding, compares her to a spirited thoroughbred, a slim graceful racing-shell, a delicately carved figurehead on an elegant ship. She in turn celebrates his manliness, potency, courage, and rugged honesty. Her role is as much that of psychoanalyst and father confessor as lover. She listens sympathetically to his detailed recollections of both wars, eases him over the rough spots, bathes his psychic injuries in the soft balm of praise, and even compares his mutilated hand to the wounds of Christ.

Were he Napoleon, Casanova, and Alexander the Great rolled into one, he could scarcely endure the weight of such extravagant praise. Cantwell bears it without the slightest embarrassment. He is hungry for it. He knows that his bad heart will give out any moment, and so takes final stock of himself and his performance in life. One would expect that now, of all times, a really critical examination would be in order. Instead Cantwell indulges in a prolonged process of ego-gratification. He encourages himself to feel superior to everyone. He is cruelly patronizing to his chauffeur Jackson, and holds the tourists in Venice in great contempt though he, too, is really an outsider in the city. He criticizes the generals in both world wars unmercifully as poor tacticians and strategists, and offers his own superior battle plans. He even sneers at President Truman. He must convince himself that he has lost none of his skill at wing shooting, brawling, loving, eating, and drinking. At last, when he has satisfied himself on all these points, he bids adieu to Renata, to Venice, and swollen with ecstasies of self-love and sublimely content with himself, dies.

Were Hemingway presenting his hero ironically, or at least dispassionately, Cantwell might have been a persuasive, pathetic portrait of an aging man trying to shore up his swollen vanity by a last fling. But Hemingway asks us to take Cantwell on his own terms, to admire him as he admires himself, and applaud his snobberies, meannesses, and undignified triumphs. The result is the precise opposite of what the author intends. Far from accepting the protagonist as presented, far from sharing Hemingway's enthusiasm for him, the reader is filled with aversion.

The novel opens with Cantwell shooting ducks in a Venetian lagoon at dawn. The scene is effectively described, but the sport is marred for Cantwell by the inexplicable surliness of his boatman. The boatman's unmotivated display of bad temper is the first emotion registered in the narrative, and it sets the tone for everything to come. It prepares us for Cantwell's own bad temper, and introduces the jarring element of abrasiveness and discord that permeates the book.

Even when he does not intend to be disagreeable, even with friends, Cantwell (like the boatman) cannot help spoiling things. The private Order of Brusadelli, which he forms with his former comrade-in-arms, the head waiter at the hotel, is an amusing bit of business, but it is immediately spoiled by Cantwell talking over the head of his friend and alienating him with an abstract discourse on military strategy. The tenderness of his sentiments even for Renata is curdled almost at once by the boastful violence of his attack on two sailors who make unflattering remarks about so young a woman being in the company of so old a man. His pet name for her is "Daughter," an especially unfortunate choice since it emphasizes the unpleasant difference of more than thirty years between them in age and brings in a disagreeable suggestion of incest that proves meaningless in the context of the novel.

A fantastic number of objects, words, and people irritate the Colonel, and he lunges out at each. His favorite epithet is "jerk," which he sprays over the whole crowded landscape of his dislikes. The novel is intended as an elegy of a dying man, bidding a last farewell to the glorious world of life. It turns instead into the peevish snarl of a dyspeptic, taking a final inventory of his distempers.

The one unspoiled aspect of the book is Venice. As Cantwell's elegy the novel may be an irritating failure. As a eulogy to Venice it is a success. Hemingway remains unmatched in descriptions of place, and when these descriptions are tinged with strong emotion, as here, they rise to the level of prose poems. Certain celebrated novels have evoked with great luminosity the cities in which they take place: St. Petersburg in *Crime and Punishment,* Paris in *The Ambassadors,* Dublin in *Ulysses.* These cities play as large a role as the characters, and often determine the course of events. Nothing so dramatic takes place in Hemingway's testament to Venice, but the Italian city on the Adriatic does emerge with lambency and clarity.

Cantwell uses foul language on almost all occasions, even in intimate conversation with Renata. The one subject in which he is free of it is the city he has come to regard as his real home. He approaches Venice with reverence. His normally rough, abrasive speech loses its coarseness and lingers lovingly, even delicately, on the lagoons, canals, marshes, islands, bridges, piazzas, and churches. The hotels, too, come in for special tributes, and even the surrounding countryside is infused with light.

Every writer has his favorite landscapes. After Paris, Venice is Hemingway's. Italy was the first foreign country Hemingway lived in. He suffered his first grievous wound there. The Italians were the first to teach him that there were modes of living outside the range of Oak Park, Illinois. Colonel Cantwell, ready to die, makes a last ritual visit to Italy. The last earthly sight he wishes his eye to rest upon is Venice, and though he is not a religious man, there is a sacramental tone about his feeling for the city. He absorbs it one final time through all his pores, and when he has gotten the whole sensory splendor inside himself, he is replete, and can die in triumph.

Venice aside, the novel misses all its targets. Cantwell is a man of furious but deformed energy. He is boastful, touchy, thin-skinned, bad-tempered, painfully self-conscious, and childish in his passion to pass all his self-imposed tests. Both he and his story read like a parody of the author, as though all the unfavorable publicity, gossip, and inflated legends about Hemingway were suddenly confirmed.

The writing, too, is nervous, rigid, and tight, itself a flagrant sign that Hemingway is not in control of his material. It was easy, almost too easy, for Wolcott Gibbs to produce a devastating *New Yorker* parody of the book, entitled "Across the Street and Into the Grill"; Hemingway had all but caricatured himself and all but written Gibbs's piece for him. *Across the River and Into the Trees* was the last of Hemingway's full-length works of fiction. If a novel can be said to reflect the novelist's private frame of mind, it was an ominous forerunner of the tensions that were to overwhelm Hemingway as the last decade of his life began.

6 THE OLD MAN AND THE SEA

The hero of Hemingway's last story is an aged Cuban fisherman named Santiago. He is more than a hero; he is a superman. Though very old, he has the physical strength of a young man and a spirit that is absolutely indomitable. Everything about him is outsized: his age, strength, his cheerful disposition, even the run of extraordinary bad luck he has at the start of the book—he has gone eighty-four days without catching a fish. When on the eighty-fifth day he does catch one, it is record-breaking, a sixteen-hundred-pound marlin, so large, powerful, and symbolic as to complete a cosmic trilogy with Jonah's whale and Moby Dick.

On several occasions Santiago is compared with Christ. His raw bleeding hands during the ordeal with the marlin recall Christ's mutilated hands. His last trip up the hill to his hut, carrying the mast on his back, is a deliberate analogy to Christ bearing his cross to Calvary. There are not enough of these resemblances to argue that the fisherman is a modern Christ and his story a retelling of the New Testament. But the connections with Jesus, half-man, half-God, are enough to draw Santiago out of a purely human frame toward the superhuman.

159

Hemingway's novels are profound inquiries into the possibilities of heroism. Most of them emphasize the obstacles to achieving it, and define the world's limitations, cruelties, or built-in evil. *The Old Man and the Sea* is remarkable for its stress on what men can do and on the world as an arena where heroic deeds are totally possible. Like Hemingway's other protagonists, Santiago is confronted with a universe filled with tragedy and pain, but these are transcended, and the affirming tone is in sharp contrast to the pessimism permeating such books as *The Sun Also Rises* and *A Farewell to Arms.*

One aspect of this universe, familiar from the earlier works, is its changelessness. The round of nature—which includes human nature—is not only eternal but eternally the same. The sun not only rises; it rises always, and sets and rises again without change of rhythm. The relationship of nature to man proceeds through basic patterns that never vary. Therefore, despite the fact that a story by Hemingway is always full of action, the action takes place inside a world that is fundamentally constant.

Moreover, its processes are purely secular in character: Hemingway's figures are often religious, but their religion is peripheral rather than central to their lives. In *The Old Man and the Sea,* Santiago is a primitive Cuban, at once religious and superstitious.

Yet neither his religion nor his superstitious beliefs are relevant to his tragic experience with the great marlin; they do not create it or in any way control its meaning. The fisherman himself relies on his own resources and not on God (in whom, however, he devoutly believes, just as Jake Barnes, while calling himself a bad Catholic, is also a devout believer). If he succeeds in catching the fish, he "will say ten Our Fathers and ten Hail Marys . . . and make a pilgrimage to the Virgen de Cobre," but these are rituals that come after the event and have no significant relationship with it.

In this universe, changeless and unaffected by divinity, everyone has his fixed role to play. Santiago's role is to pursue the great marlin. "That which I was born for," he reflects. The marlin's is to live in the deepest parts of the sea and escape the pursuit of man. The two of them struggle with each other to the death, but without animosity or hatred. On the contrary, the old man feels a deep affection and admiration for the fish. He admires its great strength as it pulls his skiff out to sea, and becomes conscious of its nobility as the two grow closer and closer together, in spirit as well as space, during their long ordeal on the Gulf Stream. In the final struggle between them, his hands bleeding, his body racked with fatigue and pain, the old man reflects in his exhaustion:

> *You are killing me, fish. . . . But you have
> a right to. Never have I seen a greater, or
> more beautiful, or a calmer or a more noble
> thing than you, brother. Come on and kill
> me. I do not care who kills who.*

On the homeward journey, with the marlin tied to the
boat and already under attack from sharks, Santiago
establishes his final relationship with the fish, that
great phenomenon of nature:

> *You did not kill the fish only to keep alive
> and to sell for food, he thought. You killed
> him for pride and because you are a fisher-
> man. You loved him when he was alive and
> you loved him after. If you love him, it is
> not a sin to kill him.*

A sense of brotherhood and love, in a world in
which everyone is killing or being killed, binds together the creatures of nature, establishes between
them a unity and an emotion which transcends the
destructive pattern in which they are caught. In the
eternal round, each living thing, man and animal, acts
out its destiny according to the drives of its species,
and in the process becomes a part of the profound
harmony of the natural universe. This harmony, taking into account the hard facts of pursuit, violence,

and death but reaching a state of feeling beyond them, is a primary aspect of Hemingway's view of the world. Even the sharks have their place. They are largely scavengers, but the strongest and most powerful among them, the great Mako shark which makes its way out of the deep part of the sea, shares the grandeur of the marlin. Santiago kills him but feels identified with him as well:

> *But you enjoyed killing the* dentuso, *he thought. He lives on the live fish as you do. He is not a scavenger nor just a moving appetite as some sharks are. He is beautiful and noble and knows no fear of anything.*

Nature not only has its own harmony and integration but also its degrees of value. In *The Old Man and the Sea* this is contained in the idea of depth. The deeper the sea the more valuable the creatures living there and the more intense the experience deriving from it. On the day that he catches the great marlin, the old man goes much farther out than the other fishermen and casts bait in much deeper water. The marlin itself is a denizen of the profounder depths. Even the Mako shark lives in the deep water and its speed, power, and directness are qualities associated with depth. There are, in fact, two orders in every species: the great marlins and the lesser, the great sharks and the smaller, bad-smelling, purely scavenger sharks who dwell in shallower water and attack with a sly indirectness in demeaning contrast with the bold approach of the Mako. There are also two kinds of men—as there have always been in Hemingway—the greater men and the lesser, heroes and ordinary humans.

Santiago is the clearest representation of the hero because he is the only major character in Hemingway who has not been permanently wounded or disillusioned. Romero, at the other end of the age scale, is the closest to him in this respect, but his disillusionment has already begun with his savage beating by Cohn and his desertion by Brett. Santiago's heroic side is suggested throughout. Once, in Casablanca, he defeated a huge Negro from Cienfuegos at the hand game and was referred to thereafter as *El Campeón*. Now in his old age, he is hero-worshipped by the boy, Manolin, who wants always to fish with him, or, when he cannot, at least to help him even with his most menial chores. At sea Santiago, sharing the Cuban craze for baseball, thinks frequently of Joe DiMaggio, the greatest ballplayer of his generation, and wonders whether DiMaggio, suffering from a bone spur in his heel, ever endured the pain to which the marlin is now subjecting him. At night, when he sleeps, he dreams of the lions he had seen, in his younger days, playing on the beaches of Africa. The constant association with the king of ballplayers and the king of beasts adds to the old man's heroic proportions.

To be a hero means to dare more than other men, to expose oneself to greater dangers, and therefore more greatly to risk the possibilities of defeat and death. On the eighty-fifth day after catching his last fish, Santiago rows far beyond the customary fishing grounds; as he drops his lines into water of unplumbed depth he sees the other fishermen, looking very small, strung out in a line far inland between himself and the shore. Because he is out so far, he catches the great fish. But because the fish is so powerful, it pulls his skiff even farther out—so far from shore that they cannot get back in time to prevent the marlin, once he is captured, from being chewed to pieces by the sharks.

> *"I shouldn't have gone out so far, fish," he said. "Neither for you nor for me. I'm sorry, fish."*

The greatness of the experience and the inevitability of the loss are bound up together. Nature provides us with boundless opportunities for the great experience if we have it in us to respond. The experience carries with it its heavy tragic price, but no matter. It is worth it.

When Santiago at last returns with the marlin still lashed to the skiff but eaten away to the skeleton, he staggers uphill to his hut, groaning under the weight of the mast. He falls asleep exhausted and dreams of the African lions. The next morning the other fishermen gaze in awe at the size of the skeleton, measure it to see by how much it is record-breaking, while the reverential feeling of Manolin for the old fisherman is strongly reinforced. Everyone has somehow been uplifted by the experience. Even on the lowest, most ignorant level, it creates a sensation. The tourists in the last scene of the story mistake the marlin for a shark, but they, too, are struck by a sense of the extraordinary.

The world not only contains the possibilities of heroic adventure and emotion to which everyone, on whatever level, can respond, but it also has continuity. Santiago is very old and has not much time left. But he has been training Manolin to pick up where he leaves off. The boy has been removed by his parents from the old man's boat because of his bad luck, but this in no way diminishes the boy's eagerness to be like Santiago. The master-pupil relationship between them suggests that the heroic impulse is part of a traditional process handed down from one generation to another, that the world is a continuous skein of possibility and affirmation. This affirming note, sub-

dued in Hemingway's earlier fiction, is sounded here
with unambiguous and unrestricted clarity.

Heightening and intensifying these already magni-
fied effects is the extraordinary beauty of nature, which
continually astonishes us with its sensuous intoxica-
tions. The account of the sea coming to life at dawn
is one of the most moving passages in the story, sup-
plemented later at rhapsodic intervals by the drama of
the great pursuit. This comes to its visual climax with
the first great jump of the marlin when, for the first
time, Santiago sees the gigantic size of his prey. Hemingway pays very close attention to the rippling and
fluting of the water, to wind currents, the movements
of turtles, fish, and birds, the rising of sun and stars.
One is filled not simply with a sense of nature's vast-
ness, but of her enchantment. This enchantment adds
an aesthetic dimension to Santiago's adventure, an adventure whose heroism invests it with moral meaning
and whose invocation of comradeship and identity
supply it with emotional grandeur.

Within this universe, where there is no limit to the
depth of experience, learning how to function is of
the greatest importance. It is not enough to have the
will to experience; one must also have technique. If
will is what enables one to live, technique is what enables one to live successfully. Santiago is not a jour-
neyman fisherman, but a superb craftsman who knows

his business thoroughly and practices it with great skill. He keeps his lines straight where others allow them to drift with the current. "It is better to be lucky," he thinks. "But I would rather be exact. Then when luck comes you are ready." To be ready, with all one's professional as well as psychological resources—that is the imperative. One reason that Hemingway's stories are so crammed with technical details about fishing, hunting, bullfighting, boxing, and war is his belief that professional technique is the quickest and surest way of getting into the sensory universe. Men should study the world into which they are born as the most serious of all subjects; they can live in it successfully only to the degree that they handle themselves with skill. Life is more than an endurance contest. It is also an art, with rules, rituals, and methods that, once learned, lead to mastery.

Furthermore, when the great trial comes, one must be alone. The pressure and the agony cannot be shared or sloughed off on others, but must be endured alone. Santiago, his hands chafed and bleeding from the pull of the marlin, his face cut, in a state of virtual prostration from his struggle, several times wishes the boy were with him to ease the strain, but it is essential that he go unaccompanied, that in the end he rely on his own resources and endure his trial unaided.

At the bottom of this necessity for solitariness, there

is the incurable reliance on the individual which makes Hemingway the great contemporary inheritor of the romantic tradition. The stripping-down of existence to the struggle between individual man and the natural world, during the course of which he rises to the highest levels of himself, has an early expression in Keats's line, "Then on the shore of the wide world I stand alone . . . ." In modern fiction it is Melville and Conrad who give this theme its most significant shape. The mysterious, inscrutable, dramatic nature into which their heroes plunge themselves in search of self-realization supplies Hemingway with the scaffolding for *The Old Man and the Sea*. Like Captain Ahab, like Lord Jim, Santiago is pitched into the dangerous ocean; for only there, and with only himself to fall back on, can he work out his destiny and come to final terms with life.

The concept of the hero whose triumph consists of stretching his own powers to their absolute limits regardless of the physical results gives *The Old Man and the Sea* a special place among its author's works. This theme of unqualified affirmation, that had begun to be struck in *Across the River and Into the Trees*, is presented here much more convincingly. Colonel Cantwell, of the immediately preceding novel, is forever talking about his heroism; Santiago acts his out. Cantwell reminisces on past triumphs; the old fisherman demonstrates them before our eyes. The strain of boastful exhibitionism that sometimes caused Hemingway to be regarded as an adolescent Byron spoiled Cantwell's story. It is almost totally absent from Santiago's.

Here we enter a world that has become, to some degree, less frightening than in the early stories. The world which injured Jake Barnes so cruelly, pointlessly deprived Lieutenant Henry of his one love, destroyed Harry Morgan at the height of his powers, and stripped Robert Jordan of his political idealism has now begun to regain its balance. It is no longer the bleak trap within which man is doomed to struggle, suffer, and die as bravely as he can, but a meaningful, integrated structure that challenges our resources, holds forth rich emotional rewards for those who live in it daringly and boldly, though continuing to exact heavy payment from them in direct proportion to how far they reach out for experience. There is no less tragedy than before, but life has lost its bleakness and accidentality, and become purposive. It is this sense of purposiveness that makes its first appearance in Hemingway's work, and sets off *The Old Man and the Sea* from his other fiction.

After the First World War the traditional hero disappeared from Western literature. He was replaced in one form or another by Mr. K., the harassed victim of the haunting, nightmarish novels of Franz Kafka. Hemingway's protagonists, from Nick Adams on, were hemmed in like Mr. K. by a bewildering and menacing cosmos. The huge complex mushrooming of technology and urban society began to smother the individual's sense of identity and freedom of action. In his own life Hemingway tended to avoid the industrialized countries, including his own, and was drawn to the primitive places of Spain, Africa, and Cuba. There, the ancient struggle and harmony between man and nature still existed, and the heroic possibilities so attractive to Hemingway's temperament had freer play. In the drama of Santiago, a drama entirely outside the framework of modern society and its institutions, he was able to bring these possibilities to their full fruition, and rediscover, in however specialized a context, the hero lost in the twentieth century.

Thus *The Old Man and the Sea* is the culmination of Hemingway's long search for disengagement from the social world and total entry into the natural. This emerges more clearly than ever before as one of the major themes in his career both as writer and man. Jake and Bill are happy only in the remote countryside outside Burguete, away from the machinery of postwar Europe. It is when Lieutenant Henry signs his separate peace, deserts from the Italian army, and retires with his love to the high Swiss mountains far removed from the man-made butchery of the war that he enjoys his brief moment of unclouded bliss. The defeated writer in "The Snows of Kilimanjaro," as he lies dying, laments his inability to free himself from the temptations of money, fashion, the life of sophisticated dilettantism, and thinks of his lost talent as resting unspoiled on the remote virginal snows cresting the summit of an African mountain (height on land is the moral equivalent in Hemingway to depth in the sea). Robert Jordan must first disengage himself from the political machinery of Spain before the act of sacrificing his life for his comrades can acquire its note of pure spiritual exaltation.

The movement away from society and its artifices is not motivated by the desire to escape but by the desire for liberation. Hemingway seeks to immerse himself totally in nature not to "evade his responsibilities" but to free his moral and emotional self. Since life in society is necessarily stunting and artificial, cowardice consists not of breaking out of it but of continuing in it. To be true to oneself makes a return to the lost world of nature imperative. And that lost world, as *The Old Man and the Sea* reveals, has its own responsibilities, disciplines, moralities, and all-embracing meaning quite the equivalent of anything present in society and of much greater value because it makes possible a total response to the demands upon the self. Santiago

is the first of the major figures in Hemingway who is
not an American, and who is altogether free of the
entanglements of modern life. It is toward the creation
of such a figure that Hemingway has been moving,
however obscurely, from the beginning. His ability
to get inside this type of character without the fatal
self-consciousness that mars so much literary "primitivism" is a measure of how far he has succeeded, in
imagination at least, in freeing himself from the
familiar restraints of convention.

In this movement from the confinements of society
to the challenges of nature, Hemingway is most closely
linked to Conrad. Conrad thrust his Europeans into
the pressures of the Malayan archipelago and darkest
Africa because he was convinced that only when removed from the comforts and protective mechanisms
of civilization could they be put to the test. In his one
London novel, *The Secret Agent,* Conrad demonstrated that suffering and tragedy were as possible in
Brixton and Camberwell as off the Java coast; heroism,
however, was not, and *The Secret Agent* stands as his
one major work that has no hero.

This embracing of nature has nothing of Rousseau
in it; it is not a revulsion against the corruption and
iniquities of urban life. It is, instead, a flight from
safety and the atrophying of the spirit produced by
safety. It is for the sake of the liberation of the human

spirit rather than the purification of social institutions that Conrad and Hemingway play out their lonely dramas in the bosom of nature.

Because *The Old Man and the Sea* records this drama in its most successful form, it gives off in atmosphere and tone a buoyant sense of release that was new in Hemingway. The story may well have been less a capstone of Hemingway's extraordinary career than a fresh emotional point of departure for the work that, because of illness and death, he was never to complete.

7 THE SHORT STORIES

While Hemingway's novels explore the nature of heroism, his short stories are devoted to loss and the resultant melancholy. Their brief incidents, single moods, isolated conversations, are perfectly suited to defining human limitations. The process of affirmation and achievement, especially in a skeptical age like the present, requires more time, detail, and preparation than the short story can naturally or comfortably embrace. The affinity between the short story and the presentation of life on the negative side is as evident in Hemingway as it is in the locked-in structure of the earlier masters, Poe, Maupassant, Chekhov, and Joyce.

Hemingway's period as a short-story writer was the fifteen-year stretch between 1921 and 1936. The stories, whether early or late, simple or complex—whether, like "My Old Man," written under the influence of Sherwood Anderson or, like "In Another Country," under the influence of James Joyce—are alike in their delineation of loss. The father in "Indian Camp," the writer in "The Snows of Kilimanjaro," the American hunter in "The Short Happy Life of Francis Macomber," the boy in "The Capital of the World," the Swede in "The Killers," lose their lives. The bull-fighter in "The Undefeated" loses his license to fight. In "Hills Like White Elephants," a couple agree to lose their baby through an abortion. The aging fighter in "Fifty Grand" loses his championship. Nick Adams, in "The End of Something," loses his first love, and in "The Doctor and the Doctor's Wife" witnesses his father's humiliation at the hands of a local lumber-jack. The boy in "My Old Man" discovers that his idolized father, a jockey, was a crook. The deep-sea diver in "After the Storm" comes within a hair's-breadth of the salvage treasure but is turned back. In "The Gambler, the Nun, and the Radio," the Mexican gambler has bad luck all the time and in all things. The aged Spaniard in "Old Man at the Bridge," victimized by the civil war, has lost everything. In "Big Two-Hearted River" the movement, to be sure, is toward life, yet the reader is tensely aware throughout that one false step on Nick's part and he will slide all the way back to the unnamed psychic nightmare he is struggling away from.

If loss can be described as a kind of death, then Hemingway's stories, at least on the surface, are pow-erfully concerned with death. This is made clear in the first collection, *In Our Time,* by the brief italicized scenes inserted between the stories. There are fourteen of them, numbered as chapters, to go with the fourteen tales, and their importance is indicated by the fact that the first edition of *In Our Time,* published in Paris, contained only these little "chapters." The stories themselves were added later in the first American edition.

The keynote of the interchapters is violence. One describes the flight of Greek refugees in the rain and mud of Thrace during the Greco-Turkish War of 1922. Another deals with German soldiers being shot one by one as they climb over a garden wall in France during the First World War. In another, six cabinet ministers are executed in the rain. In another, Nick Adams, shot in the spine, is lying near some dead Austrian soldiers in an Italian village street. In another, a soldier during a fierce bombardment frantically begs Christ to save him. In another, a policeman shoots two burglars robbing a cigar store. The last six deal with various bullfighting scenes, winding up with the death of a badly gored matador. The message is plain. In our time, the young Hemingway is saying in the early twenties, violence is the essential condition. And violence contains the threat of death in its most aggressive form.

Underneath the surface show of violence, however, there is the struggle to control it. Loss and approaching death may be the unavoidable fact of human existence. The central lesson of existence, however, is that death must be accepted, faced without demoralization, and thereby mastered. Hemingway's stories are as much a demonstration of the lesson as they are of the fact; their drama arises from the tension between them.

A superb instance of this is "Fifty Grand," where vitality and the will to endure carry Jack Brennan, the aging welterweight champion, through his ordeal. The surface of the story is gray, bleak, and forbidding. In the gritty, dirty milieu of big-time boxing, with crooked fighters, crooked managers, and crooked gamblers, Brennan has managed to survive only by being as dirty as the next man. He has a wife and two daughters who live in a normal world far away; he seldom sees them; but the longing to accumulate enough money, retire from the ring, and make his escape to them is the dream that has sustained him for years. Now his last chance has come. When approached by gamblers to throw his scheduled fight with Walcott, he agrees, bets fifty thousand of his own money on his opponent, a bet on a sure thing as he believes, and plans to retire for good.

But in the thirteenth round he is suddenly and deliberately fouled by the challenger. As he staggers back in agony, he realizes he has been double-crossed. The gamblers have secretly bet on him to win. If he falls to the canvas, the referee will award the fight to him on a foul, and he will lose his money. Though in extreme pain he manages to summon the will to go on fighting and the wit to foul Walcott with equal viciousness. Walcott does fall, is awarded the fight, and Brennan finally does make a successful escape. But at heavy cost. "I'm all busted inside," he says after the fight. Hurt though he is, he can still reflect, "It's funny how fast you can think when it means that much money."

The story is told with ruthless honesty. Brennan is a cold, surly, stingy man, and no attempt is made to sentimentalize him even though he loves his wife and children, or to idealize him even when he displays supreme courage in a moment of crisis. He lives in a harsh world, described with an extraordinary fidelity to the lingo of trainers, fighters, and their assorted hangers-on. The story is narrated by Brennan's handler and only friend in a hard-bitten, slightly melancholy tone that is perfectly suited to the occasion. Ring Lardner had been Hemingway's model for his high-school pieces. "Fifty Grand," published ten years after its author's graduation from Oak Park High School, stands comparison with any of Lardner's somber little masterpieces about sports figures. Put next to "Champion," Lardner's most famous boxing tale, it is clear that while Lardner has drawn a compelling portrait of a monster, Hemingway has drawn an equally compelling one of a man.

In the opening paragraph of "After the Storm," the first-person narrator is flat on his back being choked to death. He manages to pull a knife from his pocket and disable his attacker. Having barely averted severe damage to his person, he is next plunged into an assault on his pocketbook. As a sea salvager he is the first to reach the wreck of a liner in a quicksand off the Keys. But he cannot break into it with his light equipment. The sight of a beautiful woman with long hair floating inside the porthole makes him conscious of what treasure might lie just inches beyond his reach. He returns to shore for more tools.

A storm breaks out, however, rages for a week, and when it is over, a local Greek outfit gets out to the wreck ahead of him and picks it clean. When he arrives, there is nothing left. "First there was the birds, then me, then the Greeks, and even the birds got more out of her than I did." But though thwarted, he describes the experience with a resilience and vitality that indicate he is not crushed. He will recover from this as he recovered from the street brawl at the beginning.

"In Another Country," whose setting is Milan, has the same bitter atmosphere as "Fifty Grand," which is set in New York, and "After the Storm," which is set in Florida. The characters are men wounded in the war, taking rehabilitation exercises in a Milan hospital. The story takes place, significantly, in the autumn. It begins with a celebrated description of the cold, with night setting in early and the wind coming down from the mountains. Carcasses of dead game hang in store windows, an appropriate symbol for the mutilated soldiers who meet at therapy machines in the hospital and establish their brief relationships.

Three of them are young Italians, killers by instinct who are compared to hunting hawks. Another is the narrator, an American much like Hemingway himself at that time and place, wounded in the leg. Another is an Italian major with a withered hand who does his exercises faithfully though he does not think they will do any good. The story centers around him. The three Italians are too ferocious by nature to be within the human pale. The narrator is too young and inexperienced, too little tested, to be more than a recorder of events. It is the major, mature in years, who wills himself to life though he no longer rationally believes in it and who absorbs the catastrophic blow of his wife's sudden death without disintegrating. Even his insistence on teaching the narrator Italian grammar, in the story's one humorous moment, is a gesture in the direction of life. Again, as in most of the stories, a kernel of affirmation is disclosed inside a thick outer shell of negation.

In the wonderful early story "Soldier's Home," Krebs returns from the war later than the other veterans, to discover that civilians are now fed up with war heroes. To get any attention at all, he has to lie about his exploits, which he refuses to do. Everything else is out of joint as well. He would like a girl but the girls have all grown up and "lived in such a complicated world of already defined alliances and shifting feuds that Krebs did not feel the energy or the courage to break into it."

His parents, devout Methodists, want him to get a job, but work does not interest him. His mother wants him to pray, but he cannot; she wants him to love her, but he finds this hard to do. All emotions and emotional effort seem futile. "He did not want any consequences. He did not want any consequences ever again. He wanted to live along without consequences." Almost twenty years before Albert Camus' *The Stranger,* Hemingway has created a figure who detaches himself from everything and everyone, and is resolved to drift through life without connections, in a state of emotional neutrality—the figure who embodies for the existentialists the great heresy of nonengagement. In the end Krebs indifferently decides to get a job in Kansas City. For the moment he will go over to the schoolyard and watch his younger sister play softball.

The tone of the story is laconic, in keeping with the theme of noninvolvement. The selection of incident and detail is singularly expressive. As his mother interrupts his breakfast by saying how much she prays for him, "Krebs looked at the bacon fat hardening on his plate." Irked by the thought of the talking he must do to acquire an American girl, he remembers French and German girls with pleasure; language barriers made conversation with them unnecessary. The arrested infantilism of his life at home appears in his sister's plea that he be her beau. His response to an oppressive situation is not rebellion or resignation but withdrawal. He will leave for another town, avoid relationships, sidestep scenes and entanglements, set up a life that will go smoothly. Whether this is life or only another kind of death is less relevant than Krebs's instinct for defending himself against threatening situations. The analogies with Hemingway's own position when, at nineteen, he returned to Oak Park from the war are self-evident.

Negation also suffuses "The End of Something," which describes the unhappy moment when Nick Adams and Marjorie, their love over, part company. Two details prepare the way for the act of separation. The story begins with a brief history of the sawmill at Hortons Bay; dismantled ten years before, the area has been overrun with swampy second growth and is a mute symbol of the ravages as well as the passage of time. The two young people go fishing, but the trout do not strike. They are all around but refuse to take the bait. This, too, serves as an image of failure.

The dissolution is treated in the simplest terms, appropriate to a boy and girl in their first youth. Trying awkwardly to explain why they had better part, all that Nick can say is that it isn't fun any more. Nick and Marjorie are no Héloïse and Abelard. To verbalize their emotions beyond a certain fragmentary point would spoil the half-spoken delicacy of the parting. After Marjorie leaves, Nick's friend Bill comes along and asks him how he feels. "Oh, go away, Bill! Go away for a while," is the reply. Without answering Bill directly, Nick has amply registered the pain of the separation. The pain is nevertheless limited. The title suggests its tenuousness. The end of something—of what? The word is purposely left vague so as to lighten the relationship being ended. Nick and Marjorie are a couple of kids, and the end of their companionship, while jarring, is not tragic. The avoidance of the tragic is essential to this poignant account of human beings going away from instead of toward one another.

The Nick Adams stories are the ones most obviously connected with Hemingway's own youthful experiences. Many take place in Upper Michigan and involve Indians. Nick's father is a doctor. Like his creator, Nick hunts, fishes, and goes off by himself into the woods. He enlists in the European war and is wounded.

One of the best of these stories, "The Battler," takes place while Nick, like Hemingway, is hoboing around the country. Its principal figure is a Negro named Bugs, who spends his life taking care of a once-famous, punch-drunk ex-fighter named Ad. Nick, kicked off a freight train, runs into them at their supper fire near the tracks. He is invited to share a meal, during the course of which the fighter turns hostile and is about to attack Nick when Bugs quietly slugs him with a truncheon. Nick leaves before Ad recovers consciousness.

The Negro is beautifully portrayed, not by overt description but, typical of Hemingway, through a series of small acts that deliver their own message. He is an excellent cook: "His hot fried ham and eggs tasted wonderful." He is hospitable, insisting that Nick take some food with him when he leaves. He is gentle, polite, almost courtly. His attitude toward the man he is protecting and indeed nursing through life is deeply affectionate. For the battler's own good he must knock him out from time to time when he turns violent, but Bugs is careful to wrap the blackjack in cloth. This controlled fusion of violence and love initiates Nick into another representative moment of life.

Though obviously the hero of the occasion, Bugs is, inexplicably, a target for the author's racial slurs. Nick can tell from his voice and the way he walks that he is a Negro. His legs are described, gratuitously, as "long nigger legs." Half the time he is referred to as "nigger," half as "negro," an uncertainty on the writer's part that calls even more attention to its object. None of this is germane to the story and only smudges it. Hemingway wants to maintain a "tough-guy" realism with regard to the language of the hobo jungle, while at the same time half-recognizing that the abusive epithets are alien to the effect he wishes to produce. This is the only blemish in "The Battler," otherwise one of the most effective tales in the Nick Adams series.

The most bluntly philosophical of Hemingway's shorter tales is "A Clean, Well-Lighted Place," where the doctrine of *nada* is given an early definition. The Spanish word for *nothing* describes the universe in which man finds himself. It is blank and empty of meaning. It does not lead toward any visible end. Like the sun which rises every morning, it is always there in the same unchanging form.

The older of the two waiters in a Madrid café, the clean, well-lighted place of the title, is acutely aware of the cosmic darkness. Unmarried and living alone, he is equally aware of the importance of light. Men need an enclave of light in order to maintain themselves against the darkness. And since the darkness is formless, the lighted places must be clean and well-ordered.

The struggle of light against the dark, order against chaos, form against formlessness, is perpetual, and peculiarly human. The waiter understands the need of the ancient, deaf Spaniard who comes to the café and sits drinking night after night until closing time. The younger waiter is impatient with the old man and wants only to get home to his wife.

After closing the café, the older waiter on his way to his lodging stops in at a tavern for a nightcap. The place is well lighted, but the bar is unpolished. Light without cleanliness is not enough. "He disliked bars and bodegas. A clean, well-lighted café was a very different thing." Men need all their resources to keep from plunging back into the darkness, an element so oppressive that the waiter is moved to an ironic prayer. "Our nada who art in nada, nada be thy name."

The story ends on a note of self-mockery. Perhaps all this philosophizing about light and darkness is so much moonshine. It may be just my insomnia, thinks the waiter. It may be, but Hemingway thinks otherwise. The *nada* is unavoidably there, but so is the light, and the light can be nurtured by human effort. Inside the iron frame of nihilism, inside the gloomy aspect of things, there is place for man, room for the exercise of his energy and will.

Hemingway wrote a number of longer stories, richer

in context if not in theme than the seven relatively brief tales so far considered. Perhaps the most famous of them is "The Killers." Symbolists have had a field day with this story, seeing in it a reworking of Christian legend, with Ole Andreson (son of man) the Christ figure pursued and killed by the Devil's agents, while Nick Adams (Adam—the original man) tries vainly to prevent it.

Original man or not, Nick is once again the protagonist. He rushes off to warn Ole that the killers are after him. Andreson may or may not be Christ, but he is certainly an ex-prizefighter being chased by gangsters for having once double-crossed them. Yet it is true that in six places Hemingway says, "he turned to the wall," a variant of the Old Testament expression, to indicate that Ole is ready to die. The name of the town in the story is Summit (the peak, climax, or highest point where the ultimate confrontation takes place?). The killers are dressed exactly alike and are faceless men. Killing Ole is just another impersonal transaction to them (the absence of the human element suggesting the superhuman?). There are enough tantalizing clues in the story to encourage symbol-hunting, and if "The Killers" were not so eminently satisfactory on its own immediate terms, every reader would undoubtedly join the hunt.

But within its concrete frame no story of Heming-

way's is more satisfying. As a straightforward account
of a young man's first discovery of evil, it is powerfully
rendered. Nick has had previous experiences with
humiliation and pain. He has been slugged by a mean-
tempered brakeman and threatened by an unstable ex-
pugilist. He has seen his father faced down and has witnessed an Indian committing suicide. He has been
wounded in the war and suffered a nervous breakdown.
But he has never before encountered the face of evil
as a naked, impersonal, unavoidable, and unalterable
aspect of the moral universe, like floods and hurricanes
in the physical sphere. The two killers, precisely because they lack individuality and commit murder as a
matter of business (nothing personal intended; they
do not even know their victim), embody destructive-
ness in its purest form.

Nick is severely jarred by the experience, and the
details of the story are so arranged as to communicate
the jarring effect at every turn. The clock in the diner
does not keep the right time. The two killers wrangle
with George, the waiter, about the food and drink,
keep up a barrage of wisecracks that have a nasty
undertone, insult everyone around and even each
other, and produce a menacing atmosphere even before
they draw their guns. Nick is tied back to back with
the cook under the muzzle of a shotgun. Later he goes
off to warn Ole, who adds to his agitation by refusing

to flee or fight back or go to the police. The Swede just gives up.

Everything in the story has another face. The ordered, normal world of diners, ham sandwiches, small towns is abruptly replaced by the disordered world of gangsters and callous murder. The clock reads twenty after five, but it is really only five. The menu features chicken croquettes but all George has on hand is sandwiches. The lunch counter was not always a lunch counter; it was once a saloon. Even Ole's landlady turns out to be somebody else, a substitute taking the real landlady's place for the day. The two killers are dangerous men, yet they look like a vaudeville team. They expect Ole to appear at six; when he does not, they leave in a rage; even *their* normal routine has been upset. Ole had been a heavyweight fighter, yet he lies on his bed inert and helpless. By the time Nick gets back to the diner after his fruitless errand of warning, he no longer inhabits the same universe he did at the start. He has been inexpressibly shocked by the double discovery of annihilating wickedness and his own helplessness to do anything about it. He wants only to run away.

Before he leaves, George advises him not to think about what has happened. The advice is characteristic of Hemingway, and George's attitude throughout sets the standard. He talks back to the killers and, though bowing to superior force, never loses his dignity or nerve. His attitude contrasts with Nick's and with the Negro cook's. Nick, young and naïve, is hard hit and wants to leave town, as though he will get away from it somewhere else, as though what the killers stand for is localized. The cook wants to stay out of it altogether. George rejects noninvolvement; at the same time he keeps his balance and composure. "The Killers" is something more than a story about gangsters in the 1920s, something less than a re-creation of Christianity. It is an extraordinary account of the emotional shock that comes to all of us when we discover that the familiar world has an aspect other than the smiling and benign, an aspect of savagery and horror.

The flat, unemotional, almost unaccented tone of "The Killers" is repeated in "Hills Like White Elephants," again in the service of a large and universal theme. Here Hemingway is concerned not with the general nature of the world but with personal relationships. An American couple in Spain is waiting in a railway station for the Barcelona express that will take them to Madrid. The young woman is pregnant, and the young man is urging her to have an abortion. They discuss the matter acridly over cold beers in the extreme heat of the station. The restrained mockery, the bitterness, and the nervous pressures of their conversation light up their characters and define their feelings.

The hills in the distance remind the woman of white elephants, to which the man replies that he hasn't seen one. "No, you wouldn't have" is her tart comment. They slash at each other throughout, the man wanting her to get rid of the baby, and she concurring with bitter reluctance. "You don't have to be afraid," he assures her, "I've known lots of people who have done it." "So have I," she says. "And afterward they were all so happy." By the time the train comes, they have patched up a reconciliation on the surface, but their real feelings for one another have been badly damaged.

Their brittle, rootless life together is summed up by her rueful statement, "That's all we do, isn't it—look at things and try new drinks?" And by the description of their bags: "There were labels on them from all the hotels where they had spent nights." The man, determined to make the best of everything despite his uneasiness, thinks the two of them can still have the whole world. She denies it: "It isn't ours any more." The contrast between their condition and the normal experience is emphasized by the other travelers in the station who "were all waiting reasonably for the train." The adverb, admirably chosen and placed, suggests the ordinary world from which the couple has been separated. The story again illustrates the economy with which Hemingway manages to achieve a complex effect, in this case the exchange of a few remarks conveying all that is necessary about an involved human situation.

Still another melancholy passage is charted in "The Capital of the World," where the atmosphere of a whole city rather than the plight of two persons is evoked. The city is Madrid, and the atmosphere is a gray, lusterless one of daily disappointment and defeat. In its original magazine appearance, the story was called "The Horns of the Bull." Hemingway changed the title to shift attention away from the bullfighting episode to the wider significance of Madrid, with its frustrations, as the capital of the world.

The story covers an evening in a second-rate pension. Everyone in it suffers some kind of failure. One of the bullfighters, no longer brave in the ring, tries to make love to the chambermaid but is contemptuously rebuffed. Two country priests, in Madrid to ask a favor of the hierarchy, know they are going to be turned down. One of the waiters tries to persuade another to attend an anarcho-syndicalist meeting that night; he is unsuccessful. A new Greta Garbo movie is in town, but all Madrid is disappointed with it.

In the midst of these small mishaps, a disastrous one occurs. Paco, a young boy from the provinces training to be a waiter, boasts of his bullfighting skill. In the kitchen an older youth rigs up a chair with a pair of sharp meat knives and imitates a charging bull. In the mock fight Paco is killed by one of the plunging "horns." This dreadful accident is somehow robbed of its horror by the subtle recognition that Paco has, after all, died at the height of his illusion, that if he had grown up the chances were overwhelming that he would have been like one of the three unsuccessful bullfighters in the pension.

Or he might not have attained even that eminence. He might have become just a banderillero or a picador. But his tragedy, though the most dramatic, is not the essential one of the story; the opening line informs us that "Madrid is full of boys named Paco." There are too many like him to make his experience special. The real tragedy is the great city of which he is a small, almost indistinguishable part. It is the quality of life in Madrid, observed during a typical evening, that is the ultimate subject of "The Capital of the World."

To Manuel Garcia, the battle-scarred, middle-aged matador of "The Undefeated," bullfighting is not a glamorous dream, as it was to Paco, but a brutal reality. He is past his prime, yet insists on returning to fight though he has been badly gored not long before. Everyone urges him to quit, but stubborn professional pride drives him on. Besides, bullfighting is all he knows. He makes his comeback under the worst conditions. The promoter pays him too little and offers him a bad spot in a night program. The picadors on hand are incompetent, forcing Manuel to engage one of his own. The man he gets is his friend Zurito, the best picador in Madrid. Zurito urges Manuel not to fight again, and finally agrees to "pic" for him only when Manuel consents to quit for good if he does not perform well.

Nowhere in Hemingway, not even in the celebrated passages of *The Sun Also Rises,* is there a more compelling account of the action and drama of the bullring than in "The Undefeated." Everything is seen from the level of Manuel's eye: the invisible spectators beyond the lights, the bull in his first wild surge before being worn down to the wary uncertain animal at the end, the clever young gypsy banderillero discharging his dangerous task with incredible grace, the bored newspaper reporter taking notes from his ringside seat, and Manuel himself going through the complex exercises of his craft until, tripping over a pillow thrown by someone in the hostile crowd, he is cruelly gored. Yet he manages, with his last strength and summoning a final blaze of spirit, to kill the bull. Manuel's fighting days are over, yet in some ultimate sense he is undefeated. The pure integral soul is in his case transcendent over the limited, fallible flesh.

The story is further distinguished by the massive

presence of Zurito, one of those secondary characters who manage to control the scene though placed to one side of it. The veteran picador is not only a great man in his own field, he has a character to go with it. Though opposed to Manuel fighting again, he is willing to serve as his picador without fee. His display of strength and skill as a picador, preparing the bull properly for the muleta, is one of the few first-class touches in the evening's exhibition. He is at Manuel's side, compassionate and powerful, during all the crucial moments, in the café, the arena, and the operating table. The title of the story plainly refers to Manuel, but it may also be stretched to include Zurito.

Hemingway's uncanny deftness in rendering physical action carries over consummately into his two famous tales of big-game hunting in Africa. "The Short Happy Life of Francis Macomber," the first of these, is a superb piece of craftsmanship; as one observer put it, even the animals cooperate faultlessly. The lion and the buffalo, both wounded in the story, supply the plot with its two beautifully timed, perfectly executed climaxes. The wounded lion hides in the deep brush, waiting to spring at its assailants. The dangerous necessity of going in after it is too much for Macomber. His cowardice secretly gratifies his wife, and she proceeds to betray him that night with Wilson, the professional hunter running the safari.

The next day, angry, bitter, and ashamed, but in some curious way purged of his fear, Macomber faces up to the wounded buffalo that charges at him in a swift unexpected rush. His new-found courage releases him into happiness, but his happy life proves short, scarcely more than two seconds, for his wife, unable to bear the prospect of her husband's bravery, fires a bullet into his brain. Wilson has enjoyed her favors, but he has come to like and admire Macomber. The killing horrifies and disgusts him, though he passes it off as an accident. In Hemingway's fictional world there are many crimes but few policemen.

The story is crammed with plot, but no amount of summary can convey the acuteness with which the characters, and especially their immediate attitudes, are portrayed. The beautiful Mrs. Macomber is a parasite leeching off her husband, yet she is instantly alert to the subtlest changes in the emotional weather. Macomber is the American man-boy to the life, good-looking, likable, confused, and, though thirty-five, still groping toward maturity; when he finds it, briefly, he has an explosion of joy. And finally the third and dominant figure of the triangle, the well-tempered British guide Wilson. Like the spectator-narrators in James and Conrad, he is both inside and outside the action, taking part in it at decisive moments yet withdrawn enough from the destructive marriage of the

Macombers to comment upon it with a shrewdness and clear-sightedness that establishes a quality even more important than his courage, his intelligence. These three incisively developed figures have no trouble holding up the psychological end of a story that is already equipped with a stunning physical frame.

"The Snows of Kilimanjaro," which Hemingway declared his favorite story, is just as ambitious, but less successful. The lions and buffalo have been replaced by vultures and hyenas. The smell of death hangs over the story, not only over Harry Street's gangrenous leg but over his talent as a writer which he has murdered through self-indulgence and neglect. During his last hours he drinks, makes waspish comments to his wife nursing him in their African tent, and reminisces about his own wasted past as a writer, traveler, and soldier. In the morning the rescue plane arrives. There is room in it just for the pilot and himself. Instead of taking the direct route back, however, the plane unexpectedly flies over Mt. Kilimanjaro: "And then he knew that there was where he was going." The journey is skillfully camouflaged as an actual event. Not until it is over do we discover, with a wonderfully effective sense of shock, that the whole thing was a dream and that Harry is dead.

There are obvious parallels between Harry Street

and Hemingway. Both men idealized, even wor-
shipped, their own talent and suffered at the thought
that they might lose or dissipate it. There was an
inevitable suspiciousness in their attitude toward the
people around them, including wives and close friends,
for fear that perhaps the ability to write would be im-
paired even by the persons they loved. If Kilimanjaro
is the symbol of supreme artistic achievement, there
is the grim prospect that it can be scaled only in
fantasy. Harry reaches its summit only in his death-
dream. Finally, the places Harry touches on in his
flashback memories—Paris, the Austrian Alps, scenes
from Michigan and the American West—are straight
from Hemingway's own experience.

Perhaps because of these close analogies, the story
suffers a certain emotional distortion. The weight of
Harry's self-pity buckles the narrative frame. If Hemingway were presenting him with his usual ruthless
detachment, the self-pity would be another of Harry's
grievous faults, inevitable under the circumstances
but a weakness nonetheless. But as with Colonel Cantwell we are expected to admire him and to consider
his failures compensated for, even cancelled out, by
his rueful awareness of them. But Harry is so sorry
for himself—a sentiment that Hemingway fully shared
—it is hard for the reader to take him on his own
terms. The running quarrel with his wife seems less

like the nervous agitation of a dying man than the venom of a disappointed egotist. Harry's lament over his wasted talent goes into such ecstasies of regret that we begin wondering how genuine or deep-rooted this talent was in the first place. Wilson had warned Macomber not "to mouth it up too much." Harry Street mouths his self-concern up so much that there is little room in the story for anything else.

Not until the flight at the end above the highest peak in Africa do we emerge from the infection below, dominated by the writer's swollen leg and swollen vanity. In the epigraph Hemingway mentions the frozen body of a leopard found near the summit and remarks that no one has explained what the animal was seeking at that altitude. Harry's passage over the mountain is equally incongruous; nothing could be more earthbound than his outcries of impotence and failure. The snows of Kilimanjaro might serve as an ironic contrast to Harry's misspent life, but the irony is blurred by the constant emphasis on Harry as a gifted man led astray by a corrupting world. Neither idea seems convincing to the reader. Harry's gift seems questionable, and the world to which he succumbs, far from being corrupting, appears morally neutral, but is used by him as an excuse to justify his sense of inadequacy. Harry spends far more energy justifying his failure to become a great writer than in trying to become one. Harry's aspirations and the Kilimanjaro snows are presented by Hemingway as analogous. They are, in fact, antithetical, and the failure to recognize the actual hostility between them seriously weakens the story.

Hemingway's short fiction deals with a variety of human disasters: advancing age in "The Undefeated," the cowardice of Macomber, Harry Street's self-indulgence. Yet in these stories the process of recovery, real or imagined, is strongly suggested. Manuel's last performance has a touch of magnificence; Macomber regains his nerve; the snow-covered top of Kilimanjaro is a radiant incarnation not of Harry's corrupted hopes but of the pure ideal.

Another kind of disaster and another process of recovery are evident in "Big Two-Hearted River." What ails Nick Adams is only hinted at. In earlier tales he was wounded in the war and suffered a nervous breakdown. Now he is on a fishing trip in the woods of Upper Michigan, an expedition which in an oblique way serves as an act of healing. Nothing of any consequence happens. Nick is absolutely alone. The story is a minute record of his every physical movement. Yet the impression is subtly conveyed that each movement had better be executed just right or Nick will slide all the way back to his original breakdown. Hence there is a tension about everything he does. The act of carrying a pack on his shoulders or setting up a tent for the night or opening a can of beans is no longer a routine gesture but a psychic event. Nick is very careful and very deliberate about each step. One slip, and everything may unravel at once. Under these circumstances fishing is as risky and demanding as life. Unless grasshoppers are caught with the dew still on the grass, they cannot be caught at all. When throwing a small trout back, one must be sure not to injure its mucous membrane. The margin for error is dangerously small.

The story, like the river, is divided into two parts. In Part I Nick begins his journey on foot through a burned landscape. Everything in sight—grass, trees, grasshoppers—is blackened and sooty. There is a vague suggestion of the medieval knight passing through blasted terrain in pursuit of the Grail. The countryside ravaged by fire may be the projection of Nick's own injuries, sustained in the fiery blasting of the First World War. The most difficult and painful part of the journey is at the start. Once the country turns green again, once the healing night descends and Nick falls asleep inside his securely pitched tent, the worst is over.

Part II begins the next morning. Nick's movements are now surer and more serene. He fishes in the shallow part of the river where some of the trout are too small to be kept. But he fishes well. The sun permeates him. He is visibly emerging from the tightness and weariness of the day before. Again without any overt description of what is going on inside Nick's mind, Hemingway manages to convey what is happening there through a careful account of his gestures and movements. At the end Nick looks over at the other part of the river, the deep part where it goes through a swamp. He will fish there some day. The wish reveals how much ground he has regained. The four ancient elements—fire, earth, water, and air—fill the story. By returning to them, Nick is returning to the original primitive sources of energy which go back to the earliest myths.

The fourteen stories discussed in this chapter reflect Hemingway's mastery of the form. The terseness and brevity of his writing are the natural characteristics of the short story. It lends itself without strain to the limited emotion of sadness, which is the chief psychological residue of Hemingway's harsh view of life. Yet he manages to work into this emotion its exact opposite, the sense that all is not loss, that perhaps a meaningful though not total recovery can be made. In the novels this becomes a major theme. In the stories it is not much more than a suggestion, but a suggestion strong enough to soften their otherwise annihilative impact.

8 THE NONFICTION

Hemingway wrote three works of nonfiction. The first is his famous manual on bullfighting, *Death in the Afternoon* (1932). The second, *Green Hills of Africa* (1935), describes a big-game safari which he took with his second wife in Tanganyika. The third, *A Moveable Feast* (1964), is a memoir of his early days in Paris; it was published posthumously. Whatever their formal subject matter, the three books are rhapsodies of place. Among his other talents Hemingway was a great traveler, who made the act of travel and the countries traveled to not only attractive but supremely significant. Paris, Spain, and East Africa were among the landscapes he found compelling and, in his art, infused with magic. He returned to them again and again.

The opening chapter of *Death in the Afternoon* is an especially brilliant piece of writing. It is concise, cogent, perfectly balanced between general statement and specific illustration. It effortlessly maintains a tone that combines seriousness and informality, while covering a wide range of subjects. These include good and bad bullfights, the special reactions aroused by the

204

contrast between what one is supposed to feel and what one really feels in any given experience, and even a venture at defining morality and immorality. These themes, to be developed in detail later, are here lucidly announced.

Death in the Afternoon as a whole suggests that Hemingway had the makings of a remarkable teacher. He knows his subject, is enthusiastic about it, and expounds it clearly. The result is a model textbook. It includes excellent photographs, a glossary of technical terms, a list of the permanently scheduled bullfights, and even a bibliographical note in which the author modestly announces that his book is intended only as an introduction, that it was written because no other book in Spanish or English explained the modern Spanish bullfight both emotionally and practically, and begs the pardon of aficionados for including technical explanations with which they are already familiar. Both here and in his novels Hemingway displays all the passion of a scholar. When he wrote about anything, he was driven to learn all he could about it first. John Dos Passos, who knew Hemingway well, was struck by his intense dedication to mastering a subject: "He stuck like a leech till he had every phase of the business in his blood. He worked himself into the confidence of the local professionals and saturated himself to the bursting point."

However dedicated he may have been to bullfighting, Hemingway was timid about the didactic process
and afraid of writing a dull book. He therefore in-
jected into *Death in the Afternoon* bits and pieces of
prose that had little to do with matadors and their
difficult work. After six chapters of straight exposition, an unnamed old lady is introduced in the seventh.
While addressing what appears to be a roomful of
tourists who have just seen their first bullfight, Hemingway hears her pipe up from the back, "What is he
saying? What is that young man asking?" He promptly
begins a dialogue with her which continues off and on
for the next ten chapters. She asks a series of naïvely
blunt questions about bullfighters, which gives Hemingway a chance to depart from the strict format of
his manual and express himself freely on a wide range
of subjects, such as death, sex, and literature, only
tangentially related to the theme of his book.

The device serves several purposes: it introduces
another voice into the narrative; it keeps the writer
from sinking too far into the pure technicalities of his
subject; it gives him more flexibility in handling his
first nonfiction, an unaccustomed medium for him
after ten years devoted to novels and short stories.
The old lady holds up her end of the dialogue. She
turns out to be tough-minded, inquisitive, and sane,
facing up to the harsh facts of violent life, violent

death, and even profane language which Hemingway explores with her aid. She plays the role of straight man. Their physical contrast—he is young and male, she old and female—makes the communication between them easy, informal, and free of tension from the start. She is a dramatic novelty and a great asset to the book.

Scattered through the text are Hemingway's observations on various issues. One is his famous definition of morality: "I know only that what is moral is what you feel good after and what is immoral is what you feel bad after." This reduction of ethics to sensation is a typical pronouncement of the twenties. The traditional conviction that morality was an objective principle present in the universe, not subject to change by individual belief or disbelief, was undermined by the First World War. Millions, of course, continued to accept it and continued to regulate their lives according to it, but millions of others did not, and these set the new tone of the postwar period.

By Hemingway's definition any pleasurable experience is moral, a painful one immoral. The individual's state of mind is the sole criterion and final arbiter of morality. Bullfighting is very moral to Hemingway "because I feel very fine while it is going on and have a feeling of life and death and mortality and immortality, and after it is over I feel very sad but very fine." To those disgusted by the spectacle, bullfighting must seem profoundly immoral, as Hemingway would be the first to admit.

In an age when ethics has lost its absolute character and become relative, there is no theological supreme court to arrive at ultimate judgments. Hemingway is never more American, democratic, and egalitarian than when he asserts that one man's feelings are as valid as another's. If sensation is the test of truth, if one's capacity to react is the seat of morality, then it becomes every man's obligation to pursue sensation and exercise the capacity to respond as keenly as possible. This is exactly what Hemingway did in his life as much as in his writing. He pursued the sensations of bullfighting as far as they led. He even hoped to write a sequel to *Death in the Afternoon,* bringing it up to date twenty years later, and in 1959 was lured back by *Life* magazine for a last tour of the bullfight circuit in Spain, a tour that resulted in the articles called "The Dangerous Summer."

Since ethics is a matter of individual feeling, it is imperative to discover how one really does feel, what one's state of mind really is. Referring to the early twenties, Hemingway recalled his own initial efforts at writing honestly, at getting the emotion behind the event, at breaking through to how he really felt past the intervening layers of sham. "I found the greatest difficulty, aside from knowing truly what you really felt, rather than what you were supposed to feel, and had been taught to feel, was to put down what really happened in action; what the actual things were which produced the emotion that you experienced." He had given up journalism for literature. "I was trying to learn to write, commencing with the simplest things, and one of the simplest things of all and the most fundamental is violent death." With the wars over, the only arena left where life and death were on stark display was the bullring. This became an early focal point of his art. *Death in the Afternoon* is admittedly an expert primer on bullfighting; it is also a significant moment in Hemingway's perpetual search for aesthetic and emotional truth—and truthtelling, as he himself rigorously defined it.

The loose format of the book encourages Hemingway to indulge from time to time in eighteenth-century mannerisms, as though he were writing a novel in the style of Fielding. He had imitated Fielding in *The Torrents of Spring*. Here he interrupts the narrative to make remarks like "So you want conversation? All right, this is the end of a chapter, we can put it in." He is also encouraged to comment further on literature. Prose, he observes, is architecture, not interior decoration—an excellent thumbnail description of his own writing, with its pursuit of structural unity and distrust of ornamentation. He attacks travel books like Waldo Frank's *Virgin Spain* for their fake mysticism, always in his eyes a cover for "lack of knowledge or the inability to state clearly." He manages to get in a few thrusts at writers he does not like, T. S. Eliot, Gide, Whitman, Oscar Wilde, the New Humanists. Even Faulkner, a writer whom he praises elsewhere, is roughly treated.

The other side of his belligerence is his defensiveness. Aldous Huxley had criticized him for being ashamed of sounding cultured; in the twenties, Hemingway had frequently been attacked for being anti-intellectual and emphasizing physical toughness. Instead of ignoring such complaints or dismissing them contemptuously, Hemingway was annoyed, and looked for appropriate opportunities to hit back at his critics. He was remarkably thin-skinned. He finds room for Huxley's critical remarks in his book on bullfighting and defends himself against them at length. The necessity to justify himself was an expression of his vanity, the vanity which demanded that he always be right. It also indicated his dependence on the opinions and judgments of others. It was not enough that he do his work and let it speak for itself. It had to be defended. Despite Hemingway's professed contempt for reviewers and college professors, he obviously cared for what they thought, for what the world thought.

For all its interruptions, digressions, inserted patches of dialogue, statements on art and life, and literary feuding, *Death in the Afternoon* remains primarily a lucid, cogent, and scholarly treatise on modern bullfighting. It illustrates Hemingway's expressed belief that "as in all arts the enjoyment increases with the knowledge of the art." By increasing our knowledge of bullfighting, he hopes to increase our enjoyment of it—a scholarly objective remarkable in a writer reputed to be anti-intellectual.

The emotional aspects of the subject are given as much emphasis as the physical, and the final impressions left by the book are the feelings aroused by the bullfight. Hemingway describes the faena—the series of movements with muleta and sword ending with the death of the bull—as evoking a religious ecstasy, uniting the animal, the matador, and the spectators in a supremely passionate response that carries to an emotional level beyond death. Hemingway is also absorbed by the quality of courage, which like other qualities, he claims, has an odor of its own. It smells like smoked leather or a frozen road or the sea whipped by the wind. "But the valor of Luis Freg," says Hemingway, referring to a well-known bullfighter, "did not have that odor. It was clotted and heavy and there was a thin part underneath that was unpleasant and oozy."

In moments like these, *Death in the Afternoon*

stretches its subject to a point of maximum sensory tension. Hemingway is doing more than describing the events in the bullring, he is also defining the emotions aroused in the spectator. As in his fiction, feeling lies concealed within the action. Hemingway's purpose as an artist is to release the two simultaneously, a purpose that he pursues as ardently in *Death in the Afternoon* as in his stories and novels.

In the opening chapter of *Green Hills of Africa* someone asks Hemingway, "What do you want?" He replies, "To write as well as I can and learn as I go along." The book itself, a highly personal account of a 1934 safari, elaborates the reply. In it Hemingway discusses writing, good and bad, at length and describes in detail his own learning process as a hunter of big game. On the face of it, literature and shooting kudus in Africa seem totally unrelated. But Hemingway uses his nonfictional works as grab bags. In them he is always linking up separate ideas, no matter how dissociated they seem to be.

His remarks on literature are a thumbnail survey of the classic American writers. He finds Poe skillful but dead, Melville good but overblown. He cannot read Thoreau, and is contemptuous of Emerson, Hawthorne, and Whittier as having nice minds but no bodies. Henry James, Stephen Crane, and Mark Twain are the writers he admires. At this point he makes his famous statement that all modern American literature comes from *Huckleberry Finn*. His strong response to Twain and Crane is natural enough, but his esteem for James is surprising. James was scarcely a man of action. He dwelt less on the moment of action than on the psychological response, and his style was literary rather than colloquial. Yet he was passionately devoted to his writing, wanted to be a supreme artist, "to write as well as I can"—a devotion and ambition Hemingway shared in the highest degree. Hemingway is also gloomily convinced that for many reasons America ruins its good writers and prevents them from becoming great. He subscribes to the romantic conviction expressed by Keats and Shelley that a work of art lasts forever, long after other things have been forgotten. The problem is to get the work of art produced, despite all the pressures to the contrary.

Present also in *Green Hills* is the streak of ill temper and ill nature visible in *Death in the Afternoon*. Gertrude Stein, still unforgiven, is roughly handled. Pauline Hemingway, on safari with her husband, accuses her of jealousy and malice. This is Hemingway's cue to attack her for having lied about who taught whom to write. In truth, he claims, he was the master and Gertrude Stein the pupil. She had talent and she was nice, Hemingway adds patronizingly, until over-

come by conceit and ambition. In personal relationships Hemingway was always quiveringly hypersensitive. When Gertude Stein accused him of cowardice,
she inflicted a hurt upon him from which he was never
to recover. In *A Moveable Feast,* written twenty years
later in the 1950s, he was to return to the subject with
renewed anger and self-justification.

There are other unpleasantnesses in *Green Hills.*
The dreadful sight of a wounded hyena eating its own
intestines seems funny to Hemingway, and he dwells
upon it with relish. On another occasion, after slaying
a huge kudu bull, he admires it in death. Despite the
fatal bullet it lies unmarked. Its great sweeping horns,
heavy-maned neck, and all-round beauty extract from
Hemingway a rhapsodic tribute: "He smelled sweet
and lovely like the breath of cattle and the odor of
thyme after rain." There is something revolting about
a slayer glorifying the dead body of his deliberately
selected victim. This is a lapse not so much of morality
as of taste. To hunt is one thing. To deliver aesthetic
funeral sermons over the corpses is quite another.

Another of the book's disagreeable moments comes
in the discussion of war as a literary subject. Sitting
against a tree in Africa, Hemingway reads Tolstoy's
Sevastopol and is moved to reflect on what a major
subject war is, how important his experiences in the
Crimean war were to Tolstoy, what an advantage to a

writer, any writer, fighting in a war would be. He goes on to say: "Those writers who had not seen it [i.e., war] were always very jealous and tried to make it seem unimportant, or abnormal, or a disease as a subject, while, really, it was something quite irreplaceable that they had missed." As soon as he begins questioning the honesty of those who disagree with him, ascribing jealousy and other unworthy motives to them, his argument grows personal and loses its persuasiveness.

He forgets Dickens, Hardy, Crane, Shakespeare, Balzac, Henry James, and Dostoevsky who were never soldiers; Turgenev, whom Hemingway admires even more than he does Tolstoy, was never one either. War was scarcely irreplaceable to them. Hemingway concludes by remarking that "civil war is the best war for a writer, the most complete." This strikes a ghoulish note. Hemingway makes his observation about civil war, the most ferocious and horrifying form of slaughter, in the neutral tone of a man reporting a purely scientific fact, with no concern for the special human tragedy involved.

When he has made his comments on literature, on war, on particular writers, he gets down to the formal business of *Green Hills,* the hunting of the great kudu. His success with the one superb bull he kills is followed by an agonizing failure. After a long stalk he sights another magnificent beast. But instead of killing it, his shot only wounds it badly. The animal makes off for the hills with Hemingway and his companions in close pursuit.

The chase winds through several chapters, with the injured beast eluding the hunters who want to put it out of its misery. Hemingway is upset over shooting so poorly and inflicting unnecessary pain on one of Africa's noblest creatures. Like Wilson in "The Short Happy Life of Francis Macomber," it is a matter of honor for him to track down the kudu and dispatch it. But the animal continues to elude him and at last vanishes altogether. Bitterly disappointed, Hemingway is forced to give up the chase and return to camp. Throughout this section the writing is graphically clear, but at every point the hunter's response to the situation is stronger than the reader's. Hemingway makes his frustration and unhappiness very vivid without succeeding in getting us to share it or convincing us that the occasion is worth it. His emotion is too large for the experience that arouses it, and seems more appropriate to a human context than an animal one. If he had shot a man, he could scarcely have appeared more disturbed.

At the heart of the book is Hemingway's feeling for country. Every detail of the African landscape in *Green Hills* is treated as though it were the most precious thing in the world. "I had loved country all my life," he says. "The country was always better than the people. Natives live in harmony with the continents they inhabit, but the civilized only destroy them. They level the trees, pollute the streams, overwork the soil which turns into dust and blows away." Hemingway takes a bleak view of the United States. "Our people went to America because that was the place to go then. It had been a good country and we had made a bloody mess of it." In the end, he predicts gloomily, the whole planet may wind up like Mongolia.

But whether sandy or fertile, the earth survives. From it Hemingway, like Antaeus, drew his strength. Essentially *Green Hills of Africa* is another of his vibrant testaments to nature. It is another link in the long ecological chain that stretches from "Big Two-Hearted River" in the twenties to the sublime finale of *The Old Man and the Sea* in the fifties.

The third and last of Hemingway's nonfiction, *A Moveable Feast,* was finished a year before his death and published afterward. It recalls his years in Paris from 1921 to 1926, when he was still married to Hadley and struggling to become a writer. There are devastating portraits of Gertude Stein, Alice B. Toklas, Ford Madox Ford, Zelda and Scott Fitzgerald,

Wyndham Lewis, and some unnamed persons whom Hemingway blames for the breakup of his first marriage. While these may not take up as much actual space in the volume as other less controversial matters, the acrid impression left by them predominates.

Not all of the portraits are persuasive. One would never gather from the sketch of Ford that he had written at least two splendid novels and was a man of considerable intellectual force. Hemingway presents him as a snob and a booby. Wyndham Lewis is similarly misrepresented. Hemingway calls him the nastiest man he had ever met. His remark that Lewis had "the eyes of an unsuccessful rapist" is certainly striking, but what exactly does it mean? Again no hint is ever given that Lewis was a painter and writer of some originality.

Far better are the descriptions of the Fitzgeralds and of Gertrude Stein. Hemingway dramatizes all of Fitzgerald's weaknesses as a man, his hypochondria, alcoholism, and infantile behavior, his toleration of Zelda Fitzgerald's interference with his writing; but he is also conscious of Fitzgerald's generosity, capacity for friendship, and above all, his amazing talent. Upon reading *The Great Gatsby* early in 1925, when Fitzgerald presented him with a copy, Hemingway understood at once that in the face of Fitzgerald's creative gift, personal shortcomings were inconsequential. His discontent with Fitzgerald, his deep dislike of Zelda, were as much an expression of Hemingway's unhappiness at the invasion and waste of this gift as of his irritation with the Fitzgeralds' conduct during their association with the Hemingways. Gertrude Stein, too, is presented with a reasonable degree of complexity. Before she became overbearing, dogmatic, and increasingly intolerant of Hemingway, Miss Stein at least had displayed a great feeling for art, considerable personal charm, warmth of manner, and a genuine interest in beginning writers before this interest became tainted by the irresistible impulse to turn them into disciples.

The title of the book conveys its theme: Paris was a moveable feast, to be enjoyed everywhere in memory, almost as much as in actuality. "If you are lucky enough to have lived in Paris as a young man," Hemingway remarks on the title page, "then wherever you go for the rest of your life, it stays with you, for Paris is a moveable feast." The Paris of Hemingway's memory includes the rooms he occupied on the Left Bank with Hadley, Bumby, and F. Puss, the cafés in which he wrote his early stories, the Luxembourg Museum where he studied the Impressionist painters, the racetracks, and the apartments of Gertrude Stein and other friends. He lingers nostalgically over each of these places. They once had a special grace. Now, after thirty years, Hemingway sanctifies them in his prose.

There is a ritual tone to all this. Colonel Cantwell returns years after the event to the exact spot in Italy where he had been wounded in the First World War. He undergoes some sort of healing process by this precisely renewed physical contact. Hemingway is also returning to a significant early scene, but in memory rather than in fact, and his intention is not to heal but to immortalize. He pinpoints the Parisian places sacred to him in order to save his relationship with them from oblivion. But as in most memoirs, the result is not quite what the author had hoped for. The places, the emotions, the experiences remain less real to the reader than to him. Hemingway tries hard to convey them with the same intensity that he himself feels, and is even more careful than usual in the selection of each phrase. This produces many passages of great distinction, as good as anything he ever wrote.

Yet even in them something is missing. Not art, not skill, certainly no lack of absorption on the author's part. The missing element is, paradoxically, fiction. In *The Sun Also Rises* much less time is spent on the city than here, yet the Paris of the novel is more vivid and immediate than the Paris of the memoir. The characters in the novel live in the special atmosphere of Paris without being conscious that they are doing anything special. In *A Moveable Feast* Hemingway is im-

mensely conscious that this is the famous Paris of the
1920s just before it became famous, and that he is
Ernest Hemingway not long before he became world-
renowned. He is conscious that he is sitting in a café
in the Boulevard St. Michel in 1922, that he is writing
one of his Michigan stories, that he is poor, proud,
ambitious, and talented. His consciousness of all this
—the fame of the place, the period, and the man—
lends a note of theatricality to the occasion that, while
not exactly spoiling it, makes it inescapably artificial.
Everything seems a little posed. It is as though Hemingway stands in awe of the literary and historical importance of what he is remembering.

He cannot help being impressed by this importance.
The reader is equally impressed. It is inherent in the
subject and the occasion. The glamour of history, the
dazzle of fame, color the events just enough to keep
the book from seeming wholly natural. In a novel
these elements can be absorbed in the story or kept in
perspective by the fictional lives of characters about
whom we know nothing outside the framework of the
novel. Even Hemingway is aware of the difficulty. In a
prefatory note he suggests that the reader might want
to take the book as fiction. Under the shield of fiction,
the glare of these unavoidably glamorous recollections
might be muted, and the volume as a whole rescued
from its self-consciousness. But this remains, of course,

only a wistful hope on Hemingway's part. Our chief interest in *A Moveable Feast*—an interest nothing can really deflect—is the feeding of our curiosity about Hemingway's young manhood and the Paris of the twenties. By addressing himself to that curiosity, Hemingway cannot escape the stage-managing of his material.

In this last self-revelation Hemingway's qualities emerge more clearly than ever. He is a man of fixed purpose and great charm, highly intelligent, destructively witty, self-absorbed, convinced of his own superiority and special quality. He is also wary and suspicious, proceeding cautiously through a minefield of personal tensions, but capable of commitment and love when feeling unthreatened. Plainly visible is his immature unwillingness to accept responsibility for his actions. Though deeply in love with Hadley—she is the secret heroine of the book, the affectionate sharer of his great adventure—he blames others instead of himself for the breakup of their marriage, in an unconvincing effort to ease his painful sensation of loss.

More visible still is his will to succeed, the belligerent impulse to allow nothing to stand in the way of becoming a serious writer. Even beyond our impression of a fascinating, difficult, complicated personality driven by a violent determination to achieve, there is the overwhelming sense of Hemingway's genius—his capacity to create an instant mood, his penetrative insight into character, and above all, the verbal technique that re-creates the sensory flow in a form that somehow seems more real than the actuality of nature itself.

Hemingway was acutely aware of his own creative power and did what he could to protect it: "I always worked until I had something done and I always stopped when I knew what was going to happen next. That way I could be sure of going on the next day." And again: "I had learned already never to empty the well of my writing, but always to stop when there was still something there in the deep part of the well, and let it refill at night from the springs that fed it." The water image as a source of creativity recurs. Hemingway often felt empty after finishing a story, and found eating oysters a great restorative. Their sea taste removed his feeling of emptiness. Food, drink, sex, and writing were intertwined in a continuous circuit of energy. Maintaining this circuit, keeping it going at a high level, engaged his unflagging attention.

The connective theme among his three works of nonfiction, that keeps coming up again and again in all of them almost obsessively, is Hemingway's fierce interest in protecting his own capacity as an artist. He always returns to the question of art, good art and bad, the difference between journalism and creative writing, the difference between criticism and creative literature, good writers and bad writers, and whether one can deliberately write for money and still write well. These problems are usually the concern of college professors, for whom Hemingway professes contempt, and of literary critics, for whom Hemingway professes even greater contempt. He says to one young man in *A Moveable Feast,* " 'Look, if you can't write why don't you learn to write criticism?' " The young man, a dreadful writer, takes Hemingway's advice and goes on to become a highly successful critic. Yet Hemingway himself practises literary criticism and works as much of it as he can into his own published work.

In *Death in the Afternoon* he engaged in a long argument with Aldous Huxley over the question of how much characters in a novel ought to speak like their models in real life. In *Green Hills of Africa* he delivered himself of what amounted to a short survey of American literature. Now, in *A Moveable Feast,* he argues with Fitzgerald over whether a writer can turn out stories for the popular magazines and still retain his integrity as an artist. He has things to say about Dostoevsky, Turgenev, Tolstoy, Stephen Crane, Katherine Mansfield, Baroness Orczy, and other writers whom he was reading at the time. His comments are unfailingly interesting, often acute, and entirely the result of his own first-hand impressions. There are enough of them to indicate that Hemingway was an excellent critic, that he enjoyed exercising his critical faculties, and that his bitterness about literary criticism stemmed less from a conviction that it was an inferior art than from a natural distaste and fear of unfavorable judgments when it was directed by others against his own work.

Part of this defensiveness rose from the period. "In those days we did not trust any one who had not been in the war, but we did not completely trust any one." The credibility gap between the liberal slogans of the nineteenth century and the actuality of the First World War made the 1920s peculiarly distrustful and disillusioned. Hemingway was a supreme apostle of that distrust, which pervaded both his life and his art.

In life it helped breed in him the bristling self-protectiveness that complicated his friendships and rendered him so vulnerable to criticism. In art it made him acutely, almost obsessively conscious of "faked" emotion and "faked" writing, and elevated "true" and "truly" into the climactic words of his theorizing about style and technique. A distrust of the false, the insincere, the verbally exaggerated was stimulated in

Hemingway by the period in which he lived, and heavily influenced the creation of his deliberately deflationary, exaggeratedly underaccented and understated manner of writing. If this seemed mannered at times, if it produced artificial effects easy to imitate and parody, this only revealed the violence of his reaction against the prevailing tradition of sentimental optimism that was one of the early victims of the Great War.

Hemingway informs us in *A Moveable Feast* that he hated the name Ernest. Though he gives no reason, the name must have been grossly incompatible with his image of himself. As a word in the language, earnest came straight from the earlier tradition in which his parents were steeped. Earnestness suggests an assumption of seriousness that is not quite spontaneous or natural, with an element of strain and hence insincerity. Hemingway was serious, not earnest. He strenuously shied away from earnestness.

This small revelation is characteristic of all the other small revelations of the book. Hemingway detesting his own name, handicapping the horses at Auteuil, chattering and bantering with acquaintances at cafés, rhapsodizing on the pleasures of skiing—none of these is particularly significant in itself, yet they illuminate the man as powerfully as his relationship with Hadley, his friendships with Pound and Fitzgerald, and his observations about literature succeed in doing. *A Moveable Feast* often exposes Hemingway at his most unpleasant, yet even those who are antagonized by the sharper sides of his personality must concede the coherence, candor, and sincerity with which he presents the recollections of his romantic youth.

9 THE PURSUIT OF HEROISM

The traditional novelists, like Dickens and George Eliot, were concerned with the total personalities and social relationships of their characters. Their method was the leisurely examination and exposition of character; this included not only thoughts and behavior but manner, voice, conversation, dress, and appearance, down to the very color of the eyes.

Hemingway discarded this encyclopedic technique. Instead, he evaluated his men and women by their reaction to some deliberately contrived strain. He is interested in them only to the degree that they are under pressure, and indeed approaches them in no other way. The crisis situation, the breaking point, is his chief, almost his sole concern. His principal aim is to measure the capacity to endure under difficulties. The normal moments in life, when men function within their ordinary capacities, are scarcely present in Hemingway. It is the outer limits of energy and tension that absorb him. "Hemingway avoids the more common practical situations in life," wrote Joseph Warren Beach, "business, farming, the professions, politics, family life . . . where one is seldom confronted with life-and-death predicaments and the naked primary emotions. His people are confined mainly to occupations like sport, war, drinking, and love, where every day brings its showdown."

He is preeminently a student of the climactic moment, and the climactic moment to him is not some disaster but the response to disaster. In some cases, the misfortunes of his heroes have occurred before their stories begin. Jake's wound, the hopelessness of Robert Jordan's mission to dynamite the bridge, Colonel Cantwell's bad heart are all there at the start. How they will manage to live with calamity is the main business of the novels. Hemingway is not primarily a psychologist, fascinated by the nuances and complications of his characters' minds. He is essentially a moralist, drawing fine distinctions between the right and the wrong response. The right response is invariably the heroic one: Jake living his second-best life up to the hilt, Jordan ignoring the doom hanging over his assignment yet executing the plan perfectly, the dying Cantwell acting as though he were in perfect physical condition, Santiago determined to fish in the deepest part of the Gulf Stream despite the odds against him.

Heroism is a lonely act, and heroes are essentially lonely men. They are on a plateau by themselves, apart from others, the very quality that makes them exceptional inevitably producing their separation. Society and the social structure are almost totally absent from Hemingway's work. The individual man, in contact with at most a handful of others, is at the center of his art. To highlight this individual and provide him with an appropriate context, a small arena was indispensable. Hemingway made himself master of the small arena. The bullring where Romero puts on his magnificent display, the rickety little bridge on which Jordan concentrates all his energies, the prize ring where Jack Brennan works out the terms of his reentry into life, the small diner where Nick Adams meets the killers, are characteristic Hemingway locales.

In nearly all these works, the supreme struggle takes place inside the mind of one man. At night, when Jake cannot sleep, and the wheeling sensation goes on in his head, he wrestles with his tragic affliction. *The Sun Also Rises* is one uninterrupted flow from Jake's mind outward. The same is true of *For Whom the Bell Tolls,* where the main action takes place inside Robert Jordan's brain. All the issues of the novel are debated within himself: questions of politics, war, religion, loyalty, friendship, love, as well as specific crises, such as whether or not to kill Pablo, whether to aid the besieged El Sordo, whether to proceed with blowing up the bridge even after it is apparent it will do no good. Again the frame is miniature: the mind of one man, the small guerrilla band, the small expedition against the small bridge—a deliberately tiny area carved out by the writer from the huge structure of the Spanish civil war.

A Farewell to Arms rests on an even smaller unit, this time of only two. Frederic and Catherine build their own private shelter away from the chaos of the war. With her death the shelter collapses, and Frederic is once again where he was at the beginning, alone in the world. It was only within the private world of the lovers that he was able to realize himself. He had been a competent medic in the Italian army, but not conspicuously so, no more than others. His most astonishing feat was his successful desertion when, as one man detaching himself from the mass, he executed a spectacular escape one jump ahead of being shot.

His emotional life followed a similar pattern. At the beginning he drifts from brothel to brothel like the other soldiers, deriving only blurred satisfactions and vaguely afflicted with the memory of smoke-filled nights, one indistinguishable from another. When he meets Catherine, his aim is purely sensual, another affair that will soon meld into all the others. But, unexpectedly, it grows into something else, into a genuine passion that carries him into areas of feeling that are peculiarly his, that he can explore only on his own, and that at once sets him off from Rinaldi and the others. Thus separated from the rest of the world, the lovers create their own universe, more intense and exalted than the one they abandoned.

As an individual figure, Lieutenant Henry is less vivid than Jake or even Robert Jordan. His situation is as interesting as theirs and, outwardly, as sharply defined. He stands out in a kind of independent aloneness, much as they do. But much less takes place inside his mind than theirs. He suffers from lack of a sustaining conflict, and as a result he is mentally underemployed. His relationship with Catherine presents few emotional problems, and none that demand from him anything more than a physical response. Now and then he makes striking little comments on life, such as the parable of the ants on the burning log or the reflection about how "they always get you in the end" and if you are brave they get you sooner. Most of the time, however, he appears blank, apparently not thinking about anything.

By contrast, there is scarcely a moment when Jake and Jordan are not in the grip of intense mental activity. It is a popular misconception that Hemingway subjects his heroes only to the pressure of action. On the contrary, he subjects them to the pressure of thought as well. When there is less of this pressure as in Frederic's case, the impact of the character is visibly reduced. Frederic's sexual reactions are more potent than Jake's, yet he is the more passive figure. Hemingway is expert at describing sensory experiences. But the richness and complexity of his novels depend finally on what goes on in the minds of their central figures. The claim of *The Sun Also Rises* as Hemingway's greatest work rests in part on the density of Jake's mental and emotional life. It is not accidental that one of the writers Hemingway greatly admired was Henry James. James had little interest in pure sensation, but his concentration on the texture of mental life was phenomenal.

Though a lesser hero, Frederic still possesses a heroic quality. He has a capacity for strong emotion and responds fully to the experiences that present themselves to him. He establishes a true friendship with Rinaldi, falls profoundly in love with Catherine, creates a delicate rapport with the young priest, and later, with old Count Greffi. Though an American in a foreign army, he arouses the respect and loyalty of the Italians under him by exercising over them a firm and rational authority. He is in his own quiet and unassuming way a superior man.

Why some men are heroic and others are not is the mystery at the heart of Hemingway's work. There are born heroes like Romero who reach their summit young, and born heroes like Santiago who must wait for their great moment until extreme old age. There are the heroes who create their own heroism under stress, like Jake, Robert Jordan, and Wilson, closer to us somehow and therefore seeming the more admirable.

The nonheroic figures are, of course, far more numerous. Lady Brett and Mike Campbell have a touch of desperate glamour, but they are disintegrative creatures on the verge of collapsing into total dissolution. Margot Macomber is a straight D. H. Lawrence female, with a driving, devouring, fixated will. Robert Cohn is undermined from within by a strain of pulpy sentiment that blurs the actuality of his experiences. Even Nick Adams, the youthful protagonist of many of the early stories, remains curiously immature, never quite crossing what Conrad called the shadow-line dividing youth from manhood. In every instance, Hemingway probes for what to him is the vital element, present in some of his figures, missing in others. When the heroic response appears in unexpected places— Francis Macomber is the most striking example—the sense of discovery, of surprise, even of ecstasy however briefly sustained, becomes the climactic emotion toward which Hemingway's art has been building from the start.

Sometimes a character is barred from achieving heroism by self-pity, as with Harry Street and Colonel Cantwell. Sometimes it is marred by the author's excessive insistence on the greatness of his hero. The portrait of Santiago is weakened, though not spoiled, by Hemingway's insistence on linking him excessively with Christ, Joe DiMaggio, lions sporting on African beaches, and the gargantuan Negro whom he vanquished at hand wrestling—all giant figures whose forced connection with the old Cuban inflate him beyond his natural frame. But when a character frees himself from self-pity, as Jake does and as Robert Cohn, Lady Brett, Mike Campbell, and Catherine Barkley do not, and when Hemingway restrains himself from thrusting the heroic dimension upon his figures from the outside, the result is a purity of effect, a release of the heroic ideal that is Hemingway's supreme achievement.

In a literary period dominated by the anti-hero, Hemingway's preoccupation with heroism was a singular phenomenon. It was nevertheless highly contemporary and had little to do with traditional concepts. The men in Homer went forth to do great deeds for the sake of personal glory. The members of the Round Table performed their exploits as a kind of social service, rescuing damsels in distress and slaying dragons who were terrorizing the countryside. Don Quixote had his glorious medieval ideals, too, though the Middle Ages were over and the Knight of La Mancha, having become an anachronism, had his ridiculous aspect. The nineteenth-century heroes of Stendhal, Balzac, and Dickens went forth to seek their personal fortunes. There was the Faustian hero, present in his most modern form in the novels of Dostoevsky, Conrad, and Thomas Mann, in quest of ultimate experience.

The motive behind Hemingway's heroic figures is not glory, or fortune, or the righting of injustice, or the thirst for experience. They are inspired neither by vanity nor ambition nor a desire to better the world. They have no thoughts of reaching a state of higher grace or virtue. Instead, their behavior is a reaction to the moral emptiness of the universe, an emptiness that they feel compelled to fill by their own special efforts.

Since no support is to be expected or can be found in the cosmos, everything must come from within themselves. They are driven to set up a countervailing force that will preserve them as human beings in the face of the world's indifference, and it is this force that is the expression of their heroism. It is far more a matter of survival than of vanity, more an idealized self-preservation than an impulse to social improvement. The image of the isolated, self-contained individual poised on the brink of *nada* but saving himself through suddenly discovered tenacity and courage is a recurring one in Hemingway. The hero is not saving society or an ethical ideal or a damsel in distress. He is saving himself.

It is not his physical self that is being rescued. Nature—fertile, unchanging, eternally nourishing—sees to that. It is his emotional and spiritual self, betrayed by a universe which has lost its purposiveness, that needs rescuing, and the only rescuing agent is himself. The role once performed and since abandoned by God is now taken over by man. To preserve humanity may not be a heroic achievement for God, but it is a supremely heroic one for men. The theological vacuum left by the withdrawal of God obviously cannot be filled. Men are not gods, not in Homer and not in Hemingway. In Homer heroes were individually sponsored by the gods, which gave them a godlike aura. In Hemingway such sponsorship is withdrawn, and men are forced to sponsor themselves. They do not have a godlike aura; they are all too visibly human. Their task is not to take God's place but to learn to accept their unsupported situation without losing their nerve, without crumpling, while at the same time preserving the human values that make the effort, the strain, the whole enterprise of living worthwhile. The twentieth century is a dark, blank, mutilating age to Hemingway. His art is a complex attempt to control its effects, a passionate call to endure it bravely and humanly.

The effort extracts a certain price from his characters.

They tend to be snobbish, touchy, clannish, and nearly always in a state of tension. They are not above moments of cruelty. They are almost obsessively self-preoccupied. They live in perpetual imbalance, depending too much on themselves in a world which has withdrawn its support from them. This is self-reliance, but hardly Emerson's. It is too one-sided to fit the Emersonian concept of the individual who finds himself in a promising universe and is encouraged to great personal efforts. In Hemingway the universe is discouraging, and the great personal effort is not in responsive harmony with it but an attempt to compensate for its indifference.

Individualism in Hemingway is therefore unavoidably neurotic and tragic. It is not the optimistic American brand that believes man and the world to be made of the same improvable material. In this sense Hemingway is not only a radical individualist, but also an unwilling dualist. Physically, men and nature may be one, but on the moral and religious side the cosmos is qualitatively different from the human element. The ruptured connection between them is Hemingway's beginning premise. It was also the premise of his age, the age that lived through two world wars.

The only credible heroism is therefore anguished and painful. It is nurtured in perpetual strain and can hope for no tangible reward. Its source is the human instinct to remain human despite all pressures to the contrary. In exploring this instinct, in basing his art upon it, in creating a style reflecting its necessities, Hemingway has anchored himself in the deepest level of modern experience. When all the arguments, pro and con, about his personality, his vanity, his maturity are over, the success of this achievement will remain unimpaired.

Hemingway, though easy to label, has been hard to define. He has been called all the usual names: existentialist, realist, nihilist, romanticist, wounded idealist, Christian stoic, and tender-hearted sentimentalist hiding behind a tough exterior. There is no difficulty finding evidence from his life and work to support any of these labels, and a half-dozen others. None of them is finally satisfying or wholly accurate or more than partly applicable to Hemingway.

It is Hemingway's search for a relevant and sustainable heroism that lies at the heart of his work. This search is responsible for the profound appeal of his writing and provides the secure ground of his reputation. And that reputation, so high in its author's lifetime, will surely survive among the great reputations of American literature.

A SELECTED BIBLIOGRAPHY

By Hemingway
(Dates represent first publication in book form)

FICTION
1923   *Three Stories and Ten Poems*
1925   *In Our Time*
1926   *The Torrents of Spring*
1926   *The Sun Also Rises*
1927   *Men Without Women*
1929   *A Farewell to Arms*
1933   *Winner Take Nothing*
1937   *To Have and Have Not*
1938   *The Fifth Column and the First Forty-Nine Stories*
1940   *For Whom the Bell Tolls*
1950   *Across the River and Into the Trees*
1952   *The Old Man and the Sea*

NONFICTION
1932   *Death in the Afternoon*
1935   *Green Hills of Africa*
1964   *A Moveable Feast*

240

About Hemingway

Baker, Carlos. *Hemingway: The Writer as Artist.* 3rd ed. Princeton, N.J.: Princeton University Press, 1963.

————, ed. *Hemingway and His Critics: An International Anthology.* New York: Hill and Wang, 1961.

Baker, Sheridan. *Ernest Hemingway: An Introduction and Interpretation.* New York: Holt, Rinehart and Winston, 1967.

Callaghan, Morley. *That Summer in Paris: Memories of Tangled Friendships with Hemingway, Fitzgerald, and Some Others.* New York: Coward-McCann, 1963.

DeFalco, Joseph M. *The Hero in Hemingway's Short Stories.* Pittsburgh: University of Pittsburgh Press, 1963.

Fenton, Charles A. *The Apprenticeship of Ernest Hemingway: The Early Years.* New York: Farrar, Straus & Young, 1954.

Hanneman, Audre. *Ernest Hemingway: A Comprehensive Bibliography.* Princeton, N.J.: Princeton University Press, 1967.

Hemingway, Leicester. *My Brother, Ernest Hemingway.* Cleveland: World, 1962.

Hotchner, A. E. *Papa Hemingway, A Personal Memoir*. New York: Random House, 1966.

McCaffery, John K. M., ed. *Ernest Hemingway: The Man and His Work*. Cleveland: World, 1950.

Modern Fiction Studies (Summer, 1955). A special number devoted to Hemingway, with a checklist of criticism on his work.

Plimpton, George. "Ernest Hemingway," *Writers at Work: The "Paris Review" Interviews*. Second series. New York: Viking, 1963.

Rovit, Earl. *Ernest Hemingway*. New York: Twayne, 1963.

Sanford, Marcelline Hemingway. *At the Hemingways, A Family Portrait*. Boston: Little, Brown, 1962.

Weeks, Robert, ed. *Hemingway: A Collection of Critical Essays*. Englewood Cliffs, N.J.: Prentice-Hall, 1962.

White, William, ed. *By-Line: Ernest Hemingway. Selected Articles and Dispatches of Four Decades*. New York: Scribner's, 1967.

Young, Philip. *Ernest Hemingway*. New York: Rinehart, 1952.

INDEX

243

About the Author

Leo Gurko is professor of English at Hunter College in New York, where he teaches both graduate and undergraduate courses in twentieth-century literature. From 1954 to 1960 he served as chairman of the department. He received his B.A. from the College of the City of Detroit and his Ph.D. from the University of Wisconsin. Among his published books are *Tom Paine, Freedom's Apostle* and *The Two Lives of Joseph Conrad*. He has written many articles on modern English and American literature, particularly on Joseph Conrad, D. H. Lawrence, and Ernest Hemingway. Two of his articles on Hemingway have been frequently reprinted and one has appeared in a French translation.

Dr. Gurko has also worked as a publisher's reader, editor, and translator. He has made frequent radio and television appearances.

He enjoys playing tennis, going to the movies, traveling, and following professional baseball. He spent three separate years in Europe, one with his family on a grant from the Ford Foundation and the other two on sabbatical leave. He and his wife, herself an author of biographies for young people, divide their time between their apartment in New York City and their house in the country fifty miles away.